MW00723478

Nine Lives?:
The Politics of Constitutional Reform in Japan

Policy Studies 19

Nine Lives?:
The Politics of Constitutional Reform in Japan

J. Patrick Boyd and Richard J. Samuels

J. Patrick Boyd and Richard J. Samuels

Copyright © 2005 by the East-West Center Washington

Nine Lives?: The Politics of Constitutional Reform in Japan
by J. Patrick Boyd and Richard J. Samuels

ISBN   978-1-932728-36-1 (print version)
ISSN   1547-1349 (print version)

Online at: www.eastwestcenterwashington.org/publications

East-West Center Washington
1819 L Street, NW, Suite 200
Washington, D.C.   20036
Tel: (202) 293-3995
Fax: (202) 293-1402
E-mail: publications@eastwestcenterwashington.org
Website: www.eastwestcenterwashington.org

The *Policy Studies* series contributes to the Center's role as a forum for discussion of key contemporary domestic and international political, economic, and strategic issues affecting Asia. The views expressed are those of the author(s) and not necessarily those of the Center.

Contents

List of Acronyms

CLB	Cabinet Legislation Bureau
DPJ	Democratic Party of Japan
GS	Government Section (U.S. occupation forces)
JCP	Japan Communist Party
JDA	Japan Defense Agency
JSP	Japan Socialist Party
LDP	Liberal Democratic Party
LP	Liberal Party
MOFA	Ministry of Foreign Affairs
MSA	Mutual Security Assistance
MSDF	Maritime Self-Defense Force
NDPO	National Defense Program Outline
NFP	New Frontier Party
NPA	National Police Agency
NPR	National Police Reserves
PARC	Policy Affairs Research Council
PKF	Peacekeeping Force

PKO	peacekeeping operations
PR	proportional representation
PSI	Proliferation Security Initiative
SDF	Self-Defense Force
SDPJ	Social Democratic Party of Japan
SLOC	sea lines of communication
SNTV	single nontransferable vote
UNPCC	United Nations Peace Cooperation Corps

Executive Summary

Japan is a vibrant democracy, but its citizens have never been given, nor have they ever taken, full responsibility for authoring their own constitution—until now, that is. By the late 1990s, public opinion had shifted. A majority favor changing their constitution. And today both the ruling Liberal Democratic Party (LDP) and the main opposition party, the Democratic Party of Japan (DPJ), are preparing drafts for its revision. Japan is in the midst of one of the most consequential tests of its democratic institutions.

Although the contemporary revision debate encompasses such weighty issues as the role of the emperor, description of Japanese national character, reorganization of local government, separation of powers, and basic rights of citizens, one passage in particular continues to cast a shadow over the entire enterprise: Article Nine, the famous "peace clause" renouncing the possession and use of force for settling international disputes. Long the primary target of revisionist fervor, Article Nine was at the center of the first serious revision debate in the 1950s and controversies arising from its application helped to ignite the contemporary revision movement after the Gulf War in 1991.

There are many reasons why revision proponents have sought to change Article Nine. For some it is an impediment to the realization of national autonomy. The postwar constitution was drafted under the U.S. occupation, and Article Nine, whatever its exact origins, was one of three nonnegotiable demands imposed on the Japanese by General Douglas MacArthur. It is thus no surprise that revisionists often qualify Article Nine with the adjective "U.S.-imposed." For others the peace clause is an impediment to national muscularity. As we shall see, interpretations of the article's sweeping language have placed constraints on Japan's military and its ability to use force in foreign affairs. At times these constraints have complicated Japan's relationship with its only alliance partner, the United States, as well as efforts to increase Japanese influence in the United Nations. Finally, some favor revision because they see Article Nine as an impediment to national honesty. Following major reinterpretations in the early 1950s, Article Nine has been endlessly parsed in ways both large and small as the domestic and international political landscapes have shifted. As a result, it may be argued, Japanese security policy no longer reflects a strict interpretation of the peace clause, and the constitution should thus be brought into line with reality.

These arguments are not new. Revision proponents have advanced various versions since the 1950s. This raises two important questions. First, why has Article Nine survived so long without amendment? Second, why has the Article Nine issue returned to the political agenda with such force in recent years? More specifically: why does the LDP finally seem to have congealed on the issue, and why has the major opposition party joined in calling for constitutional revision? To address these questions, we examine evidence from the two strongest revisionist movements in postwar Japanese history: the immediate postwar period (1947–64) and the post-Cold War period (1990–present). Based on these cases, we locate the primary source of Article Nine's longevity in domestic politics. Specifically, Article Nine has found critical support from a diverse coalition driven by two very different motivations, pragmatism, and pacifism. Pragmatism refers to a particular set of beliefs used to calculate the postwar national interest in exceedingly practical (cost/benefit) terms. Applying these beliefs to the conditions facing Japan, pragmatists generated and maintained the postwar strategy of reliance on the United States to guarantee Japan's security. Pacifism, by contrast, refers to adherence to the doctrine of nonviolence. This belief spread as part of an identity movement that redefined postwar Japan as a "peace nation" (*heiwa kokka*). The policy implications of this redefinition were exemplified in a preference for "unarmed neutrality."

Although the relative strength of these two forces has varied over the years, each in its own right has been a formidable obstacle to significant change in Article Nine. Despite this long track record—and although revision is by no means a foregone conclusion—the tripartite political dynamic among pacifists, pragmatists, and those who sought to revise Article Nine has recently shifted in ways that make amendment far more likely than ever before. There has been a tremendous rise in revisionist sentiment in the political parties, the Diet, and the public. And, the pragmatist/pacifist coalition has been greatly weakened. We trace the rise of revisionism primarily to three factors: the failure of leftist parties to redefine themselves in a shifted political landscape; national and party-level institutional reforms that have strengthened the role of the prime minister within the LDP and in the policymaking process; and the leadership of the current prime minister, Koizumi Junichirō. In short, changes in partisanship, institutions, and leadership have been critical drivers behind the rise of revisionism over the last decade. International development since the early 1990s provided the revisionists with further opportunities to challenge the constitutional status quo. The rise of revisionism has enabled the Japanese government to undertake certain major policy changes as, for example, in the overseas dispatch of troops and in its Iraq policy, which is clearly a major turning point in Japan's postwar security policy.

Despite the rise in revisionist sentiment, revision of Article Nine still faces serious challenges including the failure to reach consensus among conservatives and within the LDP on many central issues relating to Article Nine, the presence of Kōmeitō in the coalition government, the politics of the main opposition party DPJ, and public opinion which is still deeply divided over collective self-defense. Consequently, the present Article Nine debate could have several possible outcomes: formalization of the informal status quo; major parties reaching an agreement on allowing a restricted form of collective self-defense; formal recognition of the right to collective self-defense without any restriction (least likely); and finally the possibility of complete failure. The study then briefly explores the likely implications of constitutional revision of the right to collective self-defense for Japanese politics, U.S.-Japan security relations, and for Japan's regional relations. In conclusion the study argues that the debate over Article Nine has shifted in ways that makes major constitutional change possible although it neither sets the future course of change nor guarantees its occurrence. Whatever the outcome, the debate will be an important, and hopefully, affirmative experience in Japanese democracy.

Nine Lives?:
The Politics of Constitutional Reform in Japan

November 2005 is the fiftieth anniversary of the founding of the most powerful institution in postwar Japanese politics, the Liberal Democratic Party (LDP). The LDP plans to mark the occasion with a party first: the release of a detailed proposal for revising Japan's constitution. Although constitutional revision has been a formal plank of the LDP platform since its establishment in 1955, and although party committees have generated recommendations for changing the constitution over the years, the LDP has never before offered the Japanese public a revision proposal with full party backing. Meanwhile the leading opposition party, the Democratic Party of Japan (DPJ), is also developing a constitutional revision proposal. When one considers that the postwar constitution has never been amended, the historical import of these developments is irrefutable. This movement among the country's leading parties comes on the heels of nearly a decade of public opinion surveys showing that a majority of Japanese favor changing their constitution. Considering these recent developments, Watanabe Osamu, a Hitotsubashi University professor who closely follows constitutional politics, declares: "Constitutional revision has now been placed on the political calendar for the first time in the postwar era."[1]

Although the contemporary revision debate encompasses such weighty issues as the role of the emperor, the reorganization of local government, the separation of powers, and the basic rights of citizens, one passage in particular continues to cast a shadow over the entire enterprise: Article Nine, the famous "peace clause" renouncing the possession and use of force for settling international disputes. Long the primary target of revisionist fervor, Article Nine was at the center of the first serious revision debate in the 1950s and controversies arising from its application helped to ignite the contemporary revision movement in the 1990s.

There are many reasons why revision proponents have long sought to change Article Nine. For some it is an impediment to the realization of national autonomy. The postwar constitution was drafted under the U.S. occupation, and Article Nine, whatever its exact origins, was one of three nonnegotiable demands imposed on the Japanese by General Douglas MacArthur. It is thus no surprise that revisionists often qualify Article Nine with the adjective "U.S.-imposed." For others the peace clause is an impediment to national muscularity. As we shall see, interpretations of the article's sweeping language have placed constraints on Japan's military and its ability to use force in foreign affairs. At times these constraints have complicated Japan's relationship with its only alliance partner, the United States, as well as efforts to increase Japanese influence in the United Nations. Finally, some favor revision because they see Article Nine as an impediment to national honesty. Following major reinterpretations in the early 1950s, Article Nine has been endlessly parsed in ways both large and small as the domestic and international political landscapes have shifted. As a result, it may be argued, Japanese security policy no longer reflects a strict interpretation of the peace clause, and the constitution should thus be brought into line with reality.

There are many reasons why revision proponents have long sought to change Article Nine

These arguments are not new. Revision proponents have advanced various versions since the 1950s. This raises two important questions. First, why has Article Nine survived so long without amendment? Second, why has the Article Nine issue returned to the political agenda with such force in recent years? More specifically: why does the LDP finally seem to have congealed on the issue, and why has the major opposition party joined in calling for constitutional revision? To address these questions, we examine evidence from the two strongest revisionist movements in postwar Japanese history: the immediate postwar period (1947–64) and the post-Cold War period (1990–present).[2] Based on these cases, we locate the primary source of Article Nine's longevity in domestic politics. Specifically, Article Nine has found critical support from a diverse coalition driven by two very different motivations, pragmatism and pacifism. Pragmatism refers to a particular set of beliefs used to calculate the postwar national interest in exceedingly practical (cost/benefit) terms. Applying these beliefs to the conditions facing Japan, pragmatists generated and maintained the postwar strategy of reliance on the United States to guarantee Japan's security. Pacifism, by contrast, refers to adherence to the doctrine of nonviolence. This belief spread as part of an identity movement that redefined postwar Japan as a "peace nation" (*heiwa kokka*). The policy implications of this redefinition were exemplified in a preference for "unarmed neutrality."

Acknowledging diverse sources of support opens the door to a better understanding of the politics of Article Nine. Focused on expanding domestic economic capacity through traditional programs of state-led development, pragmatists quickly realized the value of Article Nine as a tool for managing Japan's military alliance with the United States. Invoking the article repeatedly in security negotiations during the 1950s, pragmatists such as Prime Minister Yoshida Shigeru were able to deflect escalating U.S. demands for increased Japanese alliance contributions. And domestically they were able to leverage their support for Article Nine to attract allies on the left during crucial policy fights. As a consequence, the conservative majority in the Diet split into opposing camps of pragmatists (who supported rearmament with constraints and extreme reliance on the U.S. security guarantee) versus revisionists (who favored unconstrained rearmament and a greater degree of security independence). It is this division—not between right and left but within the right itself—that protected Article Nine in the years prior to pacifism's rise as an organized political force. In later years, this division made possible cooperation between pragmatic conservatives and pacifistic progressives in support of Article Nine's institutionalization. On numerous occasions, Article Nine found vital support both from pragmatists seeking to protect interests threatened under the U.S.-Japan alliance and from subscribers to a pacifistic identity categorically opposed to the organized use of violence. Although the relative strength of these two forces has varied over the years, each in its own right has been a formidable obstacle to significant change in Article Nine. Despite this long track record—and although revision is by no means a foregone conclusion—the tripartite political dynamic among pacifists, pragmatists, and those who sought to revise Article Nine has recently shifted in ways that make amendment far more likely than ever before. This essay seeks to explain these changes as well as their likely implications for Japan's domestic and international politics.

Before proceeding, however, a few caveats are in order. First, it is not our intention here to develop a comprehensive explanation of all the varied currents of Japan's postwar security policy. We seek to shed light on the Article Nine debate and address wider issues only to the extent they provide the necessary context for our examination of the constitutional issue. Second, although we advance what is essentially a domestic politics explanation, we do not deny the importance of the international environment in the outcomes we observe. International factors, such as the end of the Cold War, the rise of the Chinese economy, and the presence or absence of significant U.S. pressure, certainly influenced the positions of the domestic groups we examine. Our argument is not that these factors have been irrelevant to the Article Nine debate; rather, we simply contend that they have not been determinative.

Shifts in the international system have not led to shifts in Japanese security policy in any direct way. Different domestic groups have looked at the international environment and come to very different conclusions regarding the utility of Article Nine for the nation's security. That the winning coalitions emerging from these differences have so far supported Article Nine's retention is thus partly the result of international factors, but this outcome has often been at odds with the predictions of theories stressing the primacy of "third image" considerations. And although international factors have certainly contributed to recent changes in the Article Nine debate, we locate the primary drivers of this process in domestic politics. This does not mean that external events are incapable of figuring decisively in the constitutional debate in the years to come. Nor, as we shall see, does it preclude these actors from using shifts in regional and world politics to bolster their case for

no explanation of Article Nine's past, nor any assessment of its future, is complete without reference to [domestic politics]

change or stasis. Indeed, we consider several such scenarios when addressing the prospects for future change. We focus, though, on domestic politics because in our view no explanation of Article Nine's past, nor any assessment of its future, is complete without reference to the ideological differences, factional divisions, institutional arrangements, and leadership that have maintained the clause at the center of Japan's security policy for nearly sixty years.

Interpreting Article Nine

> Aspiring sincerely to an international peace based on justice and order, the Japanese people forever renounce war as a sovereign right of the nation and the threat or use of force as a means of settling international disputes.
>
> In order to accomplish the aim of the preceding paragraph, land, sea and air forces, as well as other war potential, will never be maintained. The right of belligerency of the state will not be recognized.

Understanding the nearly theological difficulties associated with interpreting these two paragraphs requires stepping back and considering both Article Nine's origins and the institutional context within which it has been contested.

Article Nine is a political manifesto, a declaration of general principle constraining state action. In this sense, it is similar to the First Amendment of the U.S. Constitution—only, instead of limiting state power vis-à-vis the citizenry, it curtails state power vis-à-vis other countries by specifying the orientation of the Japanese state in world affairs. Although the language seems unambiguous, the exact boundaries of this principle have been the subject of continuing debate, beginning with the article's very origins. One widely accepted view traces its origins to General Douglas MacArthur and his staff in the Government Section (GS) of the General Headquarters of the U.S. occupation forces (McNelly 1987: 79–80). A second view holds that the concept (and perhaps the text) was suggested to the general by Prime Minister Shidehara Kijūrō during a meeting in January 1946.[3]

A problem thus emerges in determining original intent. Following initial internal disagreements, MacArthur and the GS officers responsible for drafting Article Nine reached a common understanding regarding the principle it enshrined: nonaggression.[4] In other words, aggressive war and

Article Nine is a political manifesto...constraining state action

the possession of armaments for that purpose were renounced, but Japan retained the right to possess and exercise military capabilities necessary to preserve its existence as a sovereign nation.[5] Accordingly, "war potential" could be maintained for both self-defense and collective self-defense obligations. Shidehara's understanding of the principle, however, held that the text mandated a doctrine of state *nonviolence*. In policy terms, Article Nine forbade participation in any type of war, aggressive or defensive, as well as the maintenance of any type of military capabilities whatsoever. Although advocating that Japan entrust its security to international society, Shidehara argued that this principle precluded Japanese participation in collective self-defense arrangements since it banned the military capabilities required to meet such obligations (Schlichtmann 1995: 51–53). For most of the postwar period, interpretations have bounced between these established poles of nonaggression and nonviolence.

Article Nine is embedded in an institutional context that has greatly affected debates over its interpretation. Although the constitution explicitly grants the right of judicial review to Japanese courts, the judiciary has played a relatively small role in the Article Nine debate. In cases brought by plaintiffs charging the government with violating Article Nine, judges have seldom ruled in their favor. Instead, final judgments have not only tended to support the government's position but have also limited judicial authority vis-à-vis the other branches of government.[6] Judicial passivity in Article Nine cases remains the norm to the present day.

Due to this limited judicial role, Article Nine's institutionalization has been driven by executive and legislative action. During the long years of LDP dominance in the Diet, the de facto power to interpret Article Nine lay in the hands of cabinet politicians and an extraordinary group of bureaucrats—the legal scholars in the Cabinet Legislation Bureau (CLB). The baseline for the continuously parsed interpretations began with the CLB's 1952 definition of "war potential" (*senryoku*). Ordered by Prime Minister Yoshida Shigeru, this interpretation stated that Article Nine did not ban military capabilities falling short of the ability to conduct "modern warfare" nor the use of such capabilities to repel a direct attack (Nakamura 2001: 99). Now the use of force banned in the second paragraph was related only to the purposes of the first paragraph, which no longer proscribed self-defense. In its first formal interpretation of Article Nine, the CLB declared:

[War potential (*senryoku*)] refers to a force with the equipment and organization capable of conducting modern warfare. . . . Determining what constitutes war potential requires a concrete judgment taking into account the temporal and spatial environment of the country in question. . . . It is neither unconstitutional to maintain capabilities that fall short of war potential nor to utilize these capabilities to defend the nation from direct invasion. [Nakamura 2001: 99]

The director-general of the National Safety Agency, Kimura Tokutarō, exasperated with persistent questioning in the Diet about what constituted "war potential," finally admitted that there were "no clear quantitative measures" and appealed to "the people's common sense" (Nakamura 2001: 104). War potential, he and the CLB maintained, was definable only in relation to other states' capabilities and international conditions. It was, in effect, measurable only on a sliding scale. One man's sliding scale is another man's slippery slope.

Although this "modern warfare" standard was the subject of continuing disagreement within the CLB and would soon be revised, the assertion that such a standard existed at all was a significant innovation.[7] Moreover, the interpretation specified for the first time that Japan could use force to defend itself from attack. This was a major shift since, until the Korean War, Prime Minister Yoshida had insisted that Japan did not even have the right of self-defense under the constitution. Even after the war started, Yoshida's government had denied that the 75,000-man National Police Reserves (NPR) was responsible for external security.

Armed with this interpretation, Yoshida wielded it as a shield against U.S. demands for extensive rearmament and as a wedge to split his domestic opponents seeking to abolish Article Nine's constraints. As the Cold War progressed and U.S. demands on its Japanese partner intensified, Yoshida took full advantage of his new flexibility. By 1954, he had utilized the ambiguities of "modern warfare" to establish the Self-Defense Force (SDF)—a land, sea, and air force explicitly assigned the task of defending the country from external threats—without amending Article Nine.[8]

Following Yoshida's fall from power in December 1954, the CLB quickly persuaded the new Hatoyama government to accept an even more flexible interpretation. In this new version, the "war potential" forbidden by Article Nine was any military capability in excess of the "minimum necessary level" required to protect Japan's sovereignty from direct attacks. The new interpretation specified the conditions under which Japan could exercise self-defense: when it is facing an imminent and illegitimate act of aggression; when there is no other means of countering this act; and when the use of force in self-defense is limited to the minimum necessary level (*jiei no tame no hitsuyō no jitsuryoku*).[9] Self-defense is thus narrowly understood as only the defense of national territory (Nakamura 2001: 147).

This 1954 interpretation imposed two major constraints on subsequent Japanese security policy—or seemed to. First, it limited force levels to those sufficient to provide self-defense narrowly defined; second, it limited the use of force to self-defense. The proscription of aggressive war meant that Japan could not maintain the capability to conduct "modern warfare." Nor could it assist allied nations under attack. Although there have been a great many other twists and turns in subsequent years, there is a bottom line here: the battle for control over the definition of what constitutes "minimum necessary force" persists to this day. Political disputes over "necessary limits" (*hitsuyō na gendo*) gave way to arguments over the "necessary proper sphere" (*hitsuyō sōtō na hani*) and then "necessary minimum limit" (*hitsuyō saisho gendo*). And what is "minimum" or "necessary" in a combat situation? Hairs have been split over whether "armed force" (*buryoku*) is different from "war potential" (*senryoku*), which is clearly banned by Article Nine. Each term carries with it the weight of endlessly parsed legal interpretations. In 1968, the CLB reaffirmed that the SDF can only act "when there is a sudden unprovoked attack on Japan and there are no other means available to protect the lives and safety of the people."[10]

the battle for control over the definition of…"minimum necessary force" persists to this day

The continuous hairsplitting makes for contested politics and messy policy. Until very recently, the extant interpretation allowed an SDF officer to take any action he deems necessary to protect Japanese lives and property, but it also required him to have the approval of the prime minister. And, of course, actions of the Japanese prime minister required approval by the cabinet. And because the cabinet operates on a consensus basis, all ministers had to agree. Since the cabinet meets only twice a week, it was hard to imagine a timely authorization for a Japanese soldier who finds himself under fire.

Former Prime Minister Nakasone is only one of many prominent politicians who have criticized the impracticality of CLB interpretations. After the terrorist attacks on the United States in September 2001, he expressed his dissatisfaction with "the extreme vagueness of the term 'necessary minimum' [which] has led to very fragile constitutional interpretations and to groundless practical applications."[11] In the 2001 Antiterrorism Law, some restrictions were lifted. Now a Japanese soldier under fire has to first shout a warning. Then he has to fire in the air. Then he must fire into the ground. Then he is permitted to fire at a nonvital body part. These changes have made the interpretation more practical—after a fashion.

But perhaps the toughest problem has been the 1954 interpretation's implications for collective self-defense—namely, that it is unconstitutional.[12] This problem has driven conservative politicians mad and animated the current drive for constitutional revision. In 1951, the vice-minister of foreign affairs told occupation authorities that Japan could support U.S. troops if they were attacked on Okinawa, which was then not even Japanese territory.[13] After the 1954 interpretation and until the 1980s, however, the CLB interpreted the ban so narrowly that the SDF would not have been allowed to assist a U.S. warship that came under attack while defending Japan. In 1972, a senior CLB official explained to an upper house committee that Japan could not defend an allied country unless Japan itself was attacked.

In May 1981, the CLB issued a formal interpretation of the relationship between international law, collective self-defense, and Article Nine. This interpretation, which recognizes that Japan has the right of collective self-defense under international law but is forbidden to exercise it under Article Nine, has since been the focus of revisionists' ire. Since collective self-defense has become the centerpiece of the contemporary debate over Article Nine, this interpretation is worth quoting in full:

It is recognized under international law that a state has the right of collective self-defense, which is the right to use actual force to stop an armed attack on a foreign country with which it has close relations, even when the state itself is not under direct attack. It is therefore self-evident that since it is a sovereign state, Japan has the right of collective self-defense under international law. The Japanese government nevertheless takes the view that the exercise of the right of self-defense as authorized under Article Nine of the Constitution is con-fined to the minimum necessary level for the defense of the country. The government believes that the exercise of the right of collective self-defense exceeds that limit and is not, therefore, permissible under the Constitution.[14]

When SDF troops were dispatched to Iraq in early 2004, Prime Minister Koizumi and Japan Defense Agency (JDA) Director-General Ishiba took pains to inform other members of America's "coalition of the willing" that Japanese troops would not come to their defense if they were attacked. One can only imagine the damage that would be done to the coalition if such a situation were to occur. Even in the absence of a major incident, Dutch forces have complained about having to defend their Japanese neighbors in Samawah. When the Dutch announced their withdrawal from Iraq after twenty months of service, Koizumi asked Australian Prime Minister John Howard to send forces to take their place. Although the Howard government decided to comply, the move proved very unpopular with the Australian public.[15]

Why, then, has Article Nine never been revised? The simple answer is not wrong in this case: Article Ninety-Six of the constitution mandates that revision requires a two-thirds supermajority in both houses of the Diet and a simple majority in a national referendum. Conservatives have long complained that this bar is too high, and schemes to lower these requirements are virtually a permanent fixture within the revision move-ment. Indeed, the spring 2005 LDP draft included language that would reduce the requirement for a two-thirds supermajority to a simple major-ity of 50 percent plus one vote. Still, according to one study, Japan's amendment procedure is rated eighth out of 32 constitutional systems in level of difficulty, placing it in the same category as the United States (Lutz 1994: 360–62).

With the exception of Japan, however, all other countries with similar amendment procedures have revised their constitutions. Thus institutional difficulty may be a factor in Article Nine's longevity, but it cannot be the whole story. In fact, the more complicated answer is also the more inter-esting one. What is it about the dynamics of Japanese politics that, despite more than half a century of talk about revision, the renunciation of force to settle international disputes remains unchanged at the center of Japanese security policy? Is this because the Japanese have become recalcitrant pacifists intimidated by the ghosts of their militarist past? Is it because the left has constrained the choice of the right? Is it because Japanese national identity was transformed from "Big Japanism" to "Small Japanism" and from imperial and aggressive to mercantile and passive? These labels are all, of course, components of the conventional wisdom—and while each gets at part of the story, there remains much to unbundle.

Explaining Persistence and Change

Why has Article Nine survived unchanged for decades only to be challenged so aggressively in recent years? This section considers four possible explanations: realism, generational change, nonmajoritarianism, and antimilitarism.

Realism

Realist theories of international politics provide two possible explanations based on the ever-changing balance of power in East Asia. The first, most notably offered by Herman Kahn over three decades ago, argued that Japan, after having enhanced its power position through nearly two decades of high-speed economic growth, would seek "full superpower status," including a nuclear arsenal, in order to pursue its expanded economic interests on a global scale (1970: 153). Although Japan certainly expanded the roles and capabilities of its military in the years following this prediction, it has so far done so within the framework of Article Nine interpretations, all the while sticking closely to its alliance partner, the United States, and eschewing the acquisition of nuclear weapons.[16] Applied to explain the rise of revisionism in recent years, this realist view points to the emergence of new regional threats, such as North Korea's nuclear and missile programs and China's rapid military modernization, as having provided further incentives for the Japanese to develop a more independent defense capability. Facing these new dangers, Japan should be inclined to hedge against abandonment by the United States by introducing aircraft carriers, bombers, long-range missiles, and other weapon systems currently proscribed under the government interpretation of Article Nine.[17] This hedge is only partly operational. While the Japan Defense Agency is acquiring aerial refueling capabilities as well as assault ships with hardened decks, there is limited empirical evidence that Japan has sought a full-spectrum independent defense capability in the post-

Cold War period. Defense spending has been flat or falling for a decade, and recent government plans call for a third consecutive year of military budget cuts (Glosserman 2005). Moreover, two recent publications—a report from the Prime Minister's Council on Security and Defense Capabilities (known as the Araki Report) and the 2004 National Defense Program Guideline (NDPG)—declared the U.S.-Japan alliance to be the essential bulwark of the nation's defense. The Araki Report even called the alliance a "public good" for the region. Although realists have long predicted the development of a Japanese nuclear capability, the NDPG flatly states: "Japan will continue to rely on the U.S. nuclear deterrent."[18] Meanwhile, one draft proposal from the most revisionist party in the Diet, the LDP, recently suggested that Japan's "nonnuclear principles" be enshrined in the constitution. These are not consistently the actions of an emerging independent power.

The second alternative is subtler and thus more difficult to dismiss. The collapse of the Soviet Union, it is argued, has reduced Japan's strategic importance to the United States and thus placed pressure on Japan to increase its contributions to the alliance or risk being abandoned. Viewed as trapped in an "alliance security dilemma," Japan is predicted to increase military support for the alliance, thus requiring the revision of Article Nine's ban on collective self-defense operations.[19] This view too is problematic. First, its central assertion—that Japan's importance to U.S. security objectives in the region has declined—is debatable. Scholars argue that East Asia is the most likely location of a future great power war and the United States clearly sees North Korea and China as two of its greatest threats.[20] Significantly U.S. planners have so far addressed these threats largely by leveraging America's alliance with Japan through such measures as the Proliferation Security Initiative (PSI), the Six-Party Talks, and the recent inclusion of "the peaceful resolution of issues concerning the Taiwan Strait" among the alliance's objectives.[21] Second, although Japanese leaders and analysts have expressed concern, there is simply no evidence that the United States has ever seriously considered "abandoning" Japan (Mochizuki 1997). Third, Japanese support for softening the ban on collective self-defense has sometimes preceded and even extended beyond U.S. demands. In 2001, for example, Maritime Self-Defense Force (MSDF) officials were said to have asked their U.S. interlocutors to pressure the Japanese government to deploy Aegis destroyers to the Indian Ocean.[22]

This was an example of manufactured "foreign pressure" (*gaiatsu*) in which the real demand for change came from domestic sources.

Still, the United States is undeniably an important player in Japanese security policymaking and, by extension, the Article Nine debate. In recent years, U.S. negotiators have pushed Japan to test the boundaries of its collective self-defense ban in areas ranging from ballistic missile defense to the war on terrorism. Thus Japan's security environment—including perceived (or manufactured) regional threats and its security relationship to the United States—certainly has relevance for debates about national policy. The point here is simply that focusing solely on balances of power or on alliance demands ignores key domestic developments that are a very big part of the story—perhaps the biggest part and therefore the one we examine most closely in these pages. In our view, the rise of revisionism is due largely to recent political and institutional changes that may have permanently transformed the *domestic* balance of power between political forces invested in the Article Nine debate. Before elaborating on this position, however, we should consider some other commonly cited explanations.

the rise of revisionism is due largely to…transformed…domestic balance of power

Generational Change

Some see generational change behind the recent increase in support for constitutional revision.[23] These commentators argue that those who are too young to have known the devastation of World War II and the turbulent times that followed do not share the same commitment to Article Nine held by their elders. In this view, the rise to political power of a "postwar generation" (those now in their thirties, forties, and fifties) threatens Article Nine. But is generational change at work here? To evaluate this view, we must answer two questions. First, do differences in attitudes toward Article Nine correspond to particular age groups? And second, more specifically, do members of the postwar generation hold significantly different views about Article Nine than those of their elders?

Recent polling data provide surprisingly little evidence of generational variation—either among politicians or the public. A 2002 *Yomiuri* poll of Diet members found that those from the postwar generation favored amending the constitution at only a slightly greater rate than those from the wartime generation (72 percent vs. 68 percent).[24] A 2004 *Asahi* poll found a similarly small generational difference among the public.[25] When asked about Article Nine, however, these slight generational differences disappear. In fact, in the 2002 Diet poll, politicians in their sixties and seventies actually favored changing Article Nine at a higher rate than those in their thirties, forties, and fifties. A 2002 *NHK* poll also found no perceptible generational differences among the opinions of the public on Article Nine.[26] This result was confirmed in the 2004 *Asahi* poll, which found that Japanese in their thirties, forties, and fifties actually opposed revising Article Nine at higher rates than those in their sixties and seventies. In short, living experience of 1945 and its aftermath does not appear to be a major factor in determining people's attitudes about changing the peace clause.[27]

Nonmajoritarianism

If generational change has not strengthened the drive to amend Article Nine, then what has? Another possible explanation for Article Nine's persistence is offered by Peter Katzenstein (1996). Drawing on constructivist approaches, Katzenstein utilizes norms—collectively held understandings about social life—to explain postwar Japanese security policy. With regard to Article Nine, he argues that the constitutive norm of "procedural consultation," which identifies Japan as a "nonmajoritarian polity that respects intensely held views of strong minorities," emerged in the 1950s from the powerful threat of mass mobilization by progressives eager to avenge political defeats during the prewar period. Adopting the nonviolence view of Article Nine, this progressive minority repeatedly utilized the Diet and the courts to signal their opposition to the conservative majority's interpretation. Faced with this opposition, conservatives shelved the formal amendment effort to avoid railroading a passionate minority. No longer able to debate on constitutional grounds, conservatives and progressives then shifted the stage to informal processes wherein government interpretations became established criteria that had to be met in order to avoid further political conflict (Katzenstein 1996: 118–21).

Katzenstein's explanation is open to question on several grounds. First, the constitution requires a two-thirds majority in the Diet and a simple majority in a public referendum to be amended. Since supporters of Article Nine occupied more than a third of the seats in the national assembly for most of the postwar period, it was a legal norm, not a social one as Katzenstein contends, that necessitated the observance of nonmajoritarianism in the debate over formally revising Article Nine. Second, with reference to informal means of challenging Article Nine, Katzenstein's argument turns on the assumption that those opposing the 1954 interpretation always formed a majority. In several crucial debates, however, this was not the case. As we shall see, Ozawa Ichirō's effort to reinterpret the ban on collective self-defense and dispatch Japan's Self-Defense Force to the Persian Gulf in 1990 failed not only because of progressive opposition to the content of his proposal but also due to strong opposition from within his own party. In this crucial case, a Diet majority in fact supported the substance of the 1954 interpretation, forcing Ozawa to withdraw his draft legislation without a vote. Such cases of a majority forcing a committed minority to observe Article Nine's constraints violates Katzenstein's thesis on two dimensions: the majority and minority positions are switched (the majority *supports* Article Nine), and the result is a majoritarian outcome (the revisionist *minority* is defeated). Although Katzenstein is correct that the majority Liberal Democratic Party found ways to "normalize" relations with its opponents in the Diet following the turbulent experiences of the 1950s, the success of this effort in the Article Nine debate stemmed more from the existence of a strong support base for the peace clause within conservative circles than from mere capitulation to a vocal minority.

A third problem with the nonmajoritarian explanation is that it fails to explain a period of vital importance: the late 1990s. Following spectacular electoral defeats in 1992, 1993, and 1996, the "strong minority" of progressives Katzenstein cites supporting Article Nine was weakened as an organized political force. Thus the decline of the left during this time presents a puzzle for his theory: how has Article Nine survived in the absence of a strong minority voice? With the collapse of the "1955 System"—the stable political constellation of the ruling LDP and the permanent socialist opposition—the relationship between the ruling and opposition parties has become far more complex. In the current era of coalition governments, majoritarian outcomes have become increasingly common. Thus as the old left/right spectrum has receded in Japanese politics, nonmajoritarianism in interparty relations has lost much of its theoretical relevance to the Article Nine debate. Yet Article Nine still survives. Why?

Antimilitarism

A final explanation posits a set of culturally defined norms and perceptions constituting an aversion to the use of the military in foreign affairs. Thomas Berger argues that a "culture of antimilitarism" arose from Japanese efforts to assign meaning to their devastating defeat in World War II and became institutionalized in state structures and practices affecting security policy (1993: 131). Article Nine may thus be counted among the important institutionalized forms of this culture. The antimilitarist explanation has problems, however, when applied to Article Nine. First, as Berger concedes, Article Nine predated the emergence and consolidation of antimilitarism. Thus although antimilitarism may be asserted to have played a role in sustaining Article Nine in later periods, it does not explain Article Nine's survival during the 1950s when the nascent culture was being established.

A second problem involves the characterization of all relevant political positions as culturally driven. For example, Berger refers to a group of political centrists, led by Yoshida Shigeru, as advocates of a "merchant nation" (*chōnin kokka*) identity—a vision of a nation focusing on economic development while avoiding the pursuit of military power (1996: 336). He argues that commitment to promoting and following this identity drove Yoshida and his cohorts to establish and institutionalize the antimilitarist triumvirate of Article Nine, the SDF, and the U.S.-Japan Security Treaty. But centrists did not couch their security policy positions in identity terms, particularly in the immediate postwar period.[28] Instead they justified favored policies by emphasizing their practical consequences rather than their consistence with a particular national vision. When centrists did use identity language, it was generally to support other aspects of the postwar national order, such as the role of the emperor or the importance of democracy (Benfell 1998: 9). On the whole, in both their strategic calculus and public discourse, Yoshida and his followers focused on national interest rather than national identity.

A third problem with the antimilitarism explanation is its failure to explain the rise of revisionism in the 1990s. Berger argues that only a massive exogenous shock, such as the abrogation of the U.S.-Japan alliance in the midst of growing external threats, is capable of affecting significant change in Japanese political culture (1998: 209–10). Since revisionism has blossomed in the absence of such a shock, antimilitarism fails to explain why Article Nine is facing a serious challenge for the first time since the

1950s. We address this puzzle in the next three sections by highlighting the domestic political dynamics that have resulted in Article Nine's retention over the last half-century.

The Dynamics of Stasis: Article Nine in the 1950s

Prior to the current effort—which began after the 1991 Gulf War—there was just one sustained constitutional revision movement. Mounted in the 1950s, it was led by anti-mainstream conservatives—literally the parents and grandparents of the LDP faction in power since 2000. They failed, not because a politically constrained right was forced to acquiesce to the demands of the pacifist left, but because conservatives within the LDP were divided on the issue. To understand how Article Nine has persisted despite broad-based pressures for change, we must examine the motivations and strategies of three political groups that have battled over the constitution since the 1950s. In particular, we make two assertions. First, the strength of these warring factions has shifted over the years with important implications for Article Nine's survival. Second, despite this episodic waxing and waning, the three major groups have endured. In a precarious balancing act, two of these groups have continued to offer vital support for Article Nine. Understanding how Article Nine has persisted in the face of internal and external pressures for change is thus predicated on tracing the interaction of these groups in the policymaking process.

three political groups...have battled over the constitution since the 1950s

The first group was a collection of conservative politicians led in the immediate postwar years by Hatoyama Ichirō and, later, by Kishi Nobusuke. Many had been career politicians during the prewar years as members of the Seiyūkai party. As a result of their association with the wartime government, a large portion of the group had been forced from public life by purges during the occupation. Imbued with traditional nationalist (though not ultranationalist) sentiments, these "revisionists" held to an organic vision of Japan as a unique "national polity" (*kokutai*) distinguished primarily by its imperial institution and neo-Confucian values, which emphasize unity and sacrifice for the national order.[29] The revisionists coupled a muscular

revisionists coupled a muscular notion of national identity with realpolitik beliefs

notion of national identity with *realpolitik* beliefs emphasizing the nation's duty to ensure its own security. Accordingly they favored a combination of rearmament and conventional alliances. To achieve these ends, they called for revision of Article Nine, argued to rebuild Japan's military capabilities, and sought a reciprocal security commitment with the United States.

The second group comprised pragmatic conservative politicians led in the immediate postwar years by Yoshida Shigeru and, later, by his disciples such as Ikeda Hayato, Satō Eisaku, and Miyazawa Kiichi. Yoshida built the group through his long tenure as prime minister during and immediately after the U.S. occupation. He surrounded himself with like-minded politicians, many of whom had served with him during his days in the Foreign Ministry. Interestingly the group's vision of national identity was not significantly different from that of the revisionists. Many were devoted to the emperor and dedicated to seeing Japan reemerge among the ranks of great nations.[30] Where Yoshida and his followers differed from the revisionists was not in their understanding of national identity but in the beliefs they applied to questions of foreign policy and national development.

Pragmatist foreign policy was dominated by two ideas from the Meiji era—the notions that economic success and technological autonomy were the prerequisites of national security and that alliance with the world's ascendant power was the best means to buy time until the former could be achieved.[31] Taking cues from the Meiji oligarchs, whom Yoshida revered, pragmatists rejected focusing on military spending in favor of a broad-based plan for the state-led development of the private sector. Burdened by war devastation and cut off from traditional regional markets by the emerging Cold War, Yoshida and his cohorts departed somewhat from their Meiji model in the extent of their single-minded emphasis on the civilian economy. It is important to note, however, that they considered this strategy a temporary one.[32] In addition, as had the Meiji oligarchs, the pragmatists sought an alliance with the world's strongest power. But fearing unnecessary entanglements in Cold War superpower conflicts, they pursued an unequal alliance—one in which Japan's security was guaranteed by the United States without Japanese reciprocation.

These two groups of conservatives diverged in two important respects. First, they disagreed about the *causes* of national wealth and power. And second, they disagreed about whether Japan should be "big" or "small." Specifically, pragmatists correctly read that the United States was eager to use Japan as an "unsinkable aircraft carrier" and judged that they could hedge the risks of a U.S. alliance with a focus on commercial economic development. The unequal nature of the alliance ran counter to the *realpolitik* beliefs of the revisionists, but it did guarantee the twin goals of prosperity and security without entangling Japan in American wars. These pragmatists (sometimes called "mainstream conservatives") dominated cabinets under which all three pillars of Japan's postwar security apparatus were established: Article Nine, the Self-Defense Force, and the U.S.-Japan Security Treaty. Cabinets led by pragmatists also established such timely codicils as the "nonnuclear principles," the "arms export ban," and the "1 Percent of GNP" limit to defense spending, each of which they successfully defended from attacks by revisionists within the LDP (sometimes called the "anti-mainstream" conservatives).

Pragmatists favored retention of Article Nine because it proved useful in two ways. First, invoking Article Nine allowed pragmatists to deflect American pressure for the acquisition of military capabilities they judged unnecessary or inimical to Japan's strategic interests—defined comprehensively. Second, they found Article Nine an effective means of resisting U.S. demands for Japanese participation in international military operations. Conscious of the

> *Pragmatists favored retention of Article Nine*

difficulties of managing an alliance with a superpower, pragmatists found the ban on the exercise of the right of collective self-defense a useful means of avoiding unnecessary entanglements in American Cold War strategy. To pragmatists, Article Nine was an indispensable instrument for protecting Japanese interests within the U.S.-Japan alliance.[33]

The third group comprised intellectuals, labor activists, and leftist politicians who viewed Japan as a "peace nation" (*heiwa kokka*) and categorically opposed the use of organized violence. Initially put forward by a group of progressive intellectuals known as the Heiwa Mondai Danwakai (Peace Issues Discussion Group), the "peace nation" conception had two pillars: a commitment to peace as a supreme value and a related conviction that it was Japan's unique mission to show the world by its own example the inherent value of this commitment. Viewing security in the nuclear age as transformed, the Heiwa Mondai Danwakai argued that cooperation, rather than competition, was the strategic dynamic most likely to avoid apocalyptic wars. The mission of spreading this new logic fell to Japan as a consequence of its tremendous wartime suffering and its "natural" pacifist tendencies.[34]

The initial political bearer of this identity was a group of left-wing socialists led by Suzuki Mosaburō. Many members of the Suzuki faction had opposed the war and consequently suffered under the militarist regime. Early enthusiasts of Article Nine, members of this group were committed pacifists and adherents of the Shidehara interpretation. Shaped by their experiences and the ideas of the Heiwa Mondai Danwakai, the Suzuki faction succeeded in institutionalizing the identity in the party's "principles of peace," which called for neutralism and opposed rearmament. By the early 1950s, the Japan Socialist Party had pledged support for Article Nine and opposition to rearmament and the U.S.-Japan Security Treaty, a doctrine it called "unarmed neutrality" (*hibusō chūritsu*). Thus pacifists did not trust Japan with a full military capability, preferring instead to rely on international public opinion, diplomacy, and passive resistance to counter security threats. They expanded their grassroots networks during the 1950s and by the end of the decade had become a notable political and social force.

pacifists did not trust Japan with a full military capability

Shifts in the domestic balance of power among these three groups are at the heart of Japan's continually renegotiated compromise on Article Nine and national security policy. Until recently, each of these groups represented a significant percentage of both the political elite and the electorate. For this reason, any security policy issue required support from at least two in order to remain politically viable. In the case of Article Nine, a winning coalition was formed in the early postwar years between the pragmatists and the pacifists. Although this was an uneasy alliance across party lines, their coalition proved stable and was marked by a surprising level of cooperation. It effectively protected Article Nine from numerous challenges—especially during the turbulent and formative 1950s. In particular, this coalition proved effective in three key security policy negotiations: the U.S.-Japan Security Treaty of 1951; the Mutual Security Assistance (MSA) agreement, which led to the establishment of the SDF in 1954; and the revision of the security treaty in 1960.

Pragmatists appear to have discovered the value of Article Nine during negotiations over the U.S.-Japan Security Treaty with John Foster Dulles, the State Department representative and head U.S. negotiator. Prime Minister Yoshida entered these discussions intent on realizing his own formula for postoccupation security: (1) a treaty with the United

States guaranteeing Japan's security; (2) the establishment of a low-cost constabulary force to handle internal security matters; and (3) the provision of bases in Japan for U.S. forces. The plan reflected his concern for prioritizing commercial economic development as well as his affinity for alliances with ascendant powers. Yet it also seemed to contravene the "nonviolence" interpretation of Article Nine offered by Yoshida on numerous past occasions. As the negotiations neared, Yoshida began to withdraw from this position in order to allow Japan ready access to the important carrot of basing rights.[35]

Dulles, by contrast, sought "mutuality" in any future security relationship—a condition that to him entailed significant rearmament. Following the outbreak of the Korean War, the United States began to assert increasing pressure on Japan to rearm. At MacArthur's order, Japan established the National Police Reserves, which took over the duties of U.S. forces shifted to Korea. Although external security was not a mission of the NPR, the United States decided that Japan should be similar to Adenauer's Germany, conventionally armed and capable of engaging in collective self-defense operations within the regional theater (Dower 1979: 387–88). Yoshida responded to this pressure by arguing that U.S. demands ran counter to Article Nine and the overwhelming will of the Japanese people (Yoshida 1962: 266). By treating the matter as a constitutional issue, he injected the complications of constitutional revision into the ratification process of the proposed security pact. The invocation of Article Nine thus provided ballast for Yoshida's main practical arguments against rearmament: not only could the weak Japanese economy not bear the costs, but other countries, particularly potential trading partners in Asia, would oppose it. To maintain this position, Yoshida declared that the NPR neither violated his interpretation of Article Nine nor represented rearmament in any form.

Yoshida's use of Article Nine as a negotiating tool did not end there. After Dulles again urged rearmament in the second round of negotiations in January 1951, Yoshida secretly contacted Suzuki Mosaburō and other left-wing socialists to encourage their agitation against rearmament. Although this is the only documented case of direct cooperation between Yoshida and the left-wing socialists, one scholar asserts it is "undoubtedly the tip of the iceberg."[36] Confronted with this broadly based resistance,

the United States began to assert increasing pressure on Japan to rearm

Dulles backed down. Accepting Article Nine as the baseline for any negotiated outcome, he scaled down his demands to only a token commitment to the goal of collective security. In response, Yoshida pledged to establish a force designed for external security sometime in the near future, although he stopped short of promising a force capable of operating outside Japanese territory. In the end, Dulles concluded, "the U.S. cannot press the Japanese to assume military obligations until they have dealt with their constitutional problem" (Kataoka 1991: 93).

The negotiation over Mutual Security Assistance took place in a changed domestic political environment. Although Yoshida's pragmatist faction was still in power, it was challenged on the right by newly de-purged revisionists led by Hatoyama Ichirō following the 1952 lower house election. To guard his right flank, Yoshida had the newly reformed CLB issue the "modern warfare" interpretation of Article Nine. This move not only increased his flexibility in dealing with revisionist opponents demanding rearmament but also allowed him simultaneously to argue that the force levels demanded by the United States were constitutionally forbidden (Nakamura 2001: 99). Yoshida subsequently reached an agreement with revisionists in the opposition Progressive Party to establish a military force dedicated to maintaining external security and entered the MSA negotiations with a measure of conservative unity and Article Nine still up his sleeve.

The MSA program was an American initiative designed to exchange military and economic aid for increased military preparedness on the part of allied countries. Early on, Yoshida and his chief negotiator, Ikeda Hayato, responded to U.S. demands for increased defense efforts by reinforcing dire references to the "shallow economy" with constitutional arguments (Dower 1979: 441–42, 452–53, 461–62). In response, Vice-President Richard Nixon, frustrated by the repeated invocations of Article Nine, publicly declared the article a "mistake" during a 1953 trip to Japan (Hook and McCormack 2001: 13–14). Facing a united conservative majority, however, Dulles agreed to a compromise that provided aid in exchange for the establishment of ground, sea, and air forces with the explicit mission of maintaining Japan's external security. In May 1954, the Diet passed the MSA agreement along with legislation reorganizing domestic forces into the SDF. Both measures contained the specific stipulation that future military expansion would be in accordance with the constitution. The SDF bills were also accompanied by a Diet resolution banning the overseas dispatch of the newly created force.

The negotiations over the revision of the U.S.-Japan Security Treaty took place under a further evolving political environment. The 1955 lower house election proved a victory for both the Hatoyama group, which promised constitutional revision, and the left-wing socialists, which pledged to defend Article Nine at all costs. In the following months, the left- and right-wing socialists reunited to establish the Japan Socialist Party (JSP), while conservative forces merged themselves for the first time in the LDP. Although Hatoyama remained prime minister, the socialists for the first time obtained enough seats in the Diet to block constitutional amendments outright. These mixed electoral results reflected a growing polarization in Japanese society over the revision issue. In 1954, the left-wing socialists had joined with labor unions to establish the National Union for Constitutional Defense (Kenpō Yōgo Kokumin Rengō), an umbrella organization of political, labor, and civic groups opposed to amending the constitution. Revisionists established less influential civic action groups but nonetheless managed to produce varied revision proposals. After being initially supportive of revision throughout 1954, the media became increasingly divided. Not surprisingly, public opinion during this period showed marked ambivalence over the issue.[37]

Faced with these conditions, revisionists linked Article Nine with their effort to revise the U.S.-Japan Security Treaty. The security treaty had become increasingly unpopular in Japan during the 1950s. Criticism from both the left and the right highlighted its many "unequal" features, including the lack of an explicit U.S. security guarantee in exchange for the provision of bases. Progressives and conservatives joined to protest these status issues as infringements on national sovereignty. A second matter involved Japan's passive role in the alliance. After becoming prime minister in February 1957, Kishi Nobusuke attempted to weave these two streams of discontent into an indirect assault on Article Nine. While addressing the nagging "status" issues, Kishi hoped to introduce collective self-defense to the security relationship on at least a regional basis.[38]

Making treaty revision a central goal of his administration, Kishi sounded out Dulles on the issue in June 1957. Although Dulles rebuffed this initial request, he and President Eisenhower, who were impressed by Kishi's strong showing in the 1958 lower house election and no doubt enthusiastic about his anticommunist and revisionist credentials, eventually agreed to renegotiate the security treaty. In addition, they removed their earlier linkage of Article Nine revision with treaty renegotiation. Rather than demanding that Kishi expend the tremendous political capital necessary to revise Article Nine prior to treaty negotiations, Dulles instead offered him an opportunity to score a relatively easy political victory. Such a victory might elevate Kishi's domestic stature and thus increase his future effectiveness in bringing about constitutional change and a collective self-defense arrangement.[39]

Whatever his long-term ambitions, Kishi lacked the votes to pass a treaty revision that challenged the constitutional status quo during this period. Pragmatists were now joined by a sizable group of pacifists in supporting Article Nine. Yoshida, who maintained influence through his trusted lieutenants Ikeda Hayato and Satō Eisaku, continued to restrain fervor for constitutional revision within the LDP, while Suzuki Mosaburō now led a pacifist-dominated JSP holding more than 35 percent of the seats in the House of Representatives. Even in the LDP, only the Kishi and Ishii factions could be considered thoroughly revisionist at this time (Fukui 1970: 221). Moreover, with the removal of the constitutional dimension from the treaty negotiations, the socialists called for the abrogation of the treaty and pragmatists and revisionists alike had become cool to the entire enterprise.

Two factors explain this unexpected opposition. First, the escalation of tensions between the United States and China in the Taiwan Straits beginning in August 1958 accentuated Article Nine's value as a means of avoiding Japanese entrapment in a future conflict. Faced with the possibility of being "drawn into" (*makikomareru*) a regional war likely to harm Japan's interests, pragmatists balked at handing a political victory to revisionist Kishi, and even other revisionists began to have second thoughts. In the wake of the militarized dispute in the Taiwan Straits, for example, Kōno Ichirō, a revisionist and key Kishi ally in the LDP, began to argue that constitutional revision was "ideal but impossible" (Kataoka 1991: 194–96). Second, the position of the left wing within the JSP was strengthened when Kishi introduced legislation to enhance the powers of the police. Viewing this as a strategy to suppress their movement, the socialists unified around an anti-Kishi platform calling for abrogation of the security treaty and opposing treaty revision. After Kishi told a foreign reporter he hoped eventually to "abrogate" Article Nine, the JSP intensified its efforts to defeat both the new police legislation and the treaty revision.[40]

The remainder of the treaty revision episode became a cautionary tale for the revision movement. Pragmatists and pacifists first joined to force Kishi to table his police legislation in November 1958. The next eighteen months saw the largest mass protests in Japan's postwar history, organized by the National Congress for Opposition to the Security Treaty, a coalition of leftist political parties, labor unions, student organizations, and civic action groups. Yoshida and the pragmatists, meanwhile, continued to withhold their support for treaty revision until Kishi agreed to name Ikeda as his successor in December 1959 (Kataoka 1991: 199–200). During the Diet debate that followed the treaty signing in January 1960, Kishi and his foreign minister repeatedly acknowledged the ban on collective self-defense under fierce questioning from both the opposition and members of their own party. The spectacle of staunch revisionists invoking Article Nine for strategic and political advantage would be duplicated in ensuing decades—up to and including Japan's dispatch of troops to Iraq in 2004.[41]

The episode reached a crescendo in May 1960 when Kishi forced the revised treaty through the Diet despite the JSP's obstructionist tactics. During the following week, the media condemned Kishi's action, while an unprecedented number of mass demonstrations and strikes were held in opposition to the treaty. The combined onslaught forced Kishi to cancel a scheduled visit by Eisenhower and eventually to resign as prime minister in June. Ikeda succeeded him as prime minister, returning the mainstream conservatives to power. Although the new treaty became law, the joint efforts of pragmatist factions within the LDP and the pacifist left succeeded in unseating Kishi and averting constitutional revision. In 1964, when a commission created by the Diet to consider constitutional issues submitted a final report in which the majority of commissioners backed revising Article Nine, Ikeda simply ignored it (Ward 1965: 408–25).

In the years between 1947 and 1954, when the core structures of Japan's postwar security system were established, pragmatists were indispensable to the retention of Article Nine. During this period, de-purged revisionists returned to public life in great numbers, pacifists were weakly organized within the socialist movement, the United States placed direct pressure on Japan to revise the constitution, and both the public and media remained open to rearmament and constitutional revision.

pragmatists were indispensable to the retention of Article Nine

Although assessing counterfactuals is not an exact science, these factors point to the decisive significance of pragmatism for Article Nine's survival. Pragmatists established Article Nine as the central weapon against expansive U.S. demands during security negotiations, resurrected the CLB to create and maintain interpretations useful for this purpose, and covertly cooperated with pacifists on the left. The combined result of these acts frustrated revisionists at home and abroad by strengthening Article Nine's place in the institutional structure and political discourse.

Article Nine's persistence after 1954, however, reflects the contributions of both pragmatism and pacifism. By mid-decade, a single pacifist-dominated party was able to block any attempt at formal amendment of the constitution. Pacifists' reliance on extraparliamentary tactics helped spread the "peace nation" identity to a broad set of social actors. Although they were incapable of stopping regular legislation through normal parliamentary procedures, their use of obstructionist tactics proved effective on occasion (Packard 1966: 101–5). Pragmatists too played a significant role. The CLB continued to keep vigilant watch over Yoshida's interpretation, even during revisionist administrations. More important, the large number of pragmatists within the LDP constrained revisionists while also maintaining their power position within the intraparty factional balance (Fukui 1970: 225–26). It is this deep internal division—between revisionists and pragmatists—within the dominant conservative party that most protected Article Nine from formal change during this time. Without it the coalition of pragmatists and pacifists in support of Article Nine would not have been possible. During the late 1950s, this coalition proved decisive in delivering legislative defeats that weakened revisionist influence and frustrated the constitutional revision project. This was also the case in negotiations with the United States. In one remembrance, former Yoshida lieutenant Miyazawa Kiichi praised the effectiveness of coupling Article Nine with the threat of the pacifist left as a bargaining tactic and argued that this combination proved decisive in enabling Japan to avoid unnecessary concessions in the bilateral negations of this period. In this way, he concedes that the pacifists were useful adversaries during the 1950s (Miyazawa 1997: 12).

War and Peacekeeping: Article Nine in the 1990s

Despite monumental structural shifts since 1960—particularly the rise of the Japanese economy—Article Nine and the 1954 interpretation survived the next three decades without significant change. The decade of the 1990s, however, brought with it international and domestic pressures that have given new life to the constitutional debate in general and the drive to revise Article Nine in particular. More important, changes have occurred in the way the government applies Article Nine and in the relative power of the three groups involved in the debate.

international and domestic pressures [gave] new life to the constitutional debate

The three groups assumed their customary roles in the first major security crisis of the period, the 1991 Gulf War. Following Iraq's invasion of Kuwait, the United States placed intense pressure on the administration of Kaifu Toshiki to provide financing and personnel for the international effort to liberate the Gulf Coast state. The Kaifu government was divided between pragmatists and revisionists. Kaifu, a pragmatist, was head of a small faction and needed the support of others to remain in office. As a result, Japan's initial response was driven by a small group of revisionists—led by LDP Secretary-General Ozawa Ichirō—who held high factional and party posts but were not cabinet members.[42] Ozawa and his allies put forward the United Nations Peace Cooperation Corps (UNPCC) bill, which called for a small contingent of lightly armed SDF members to be dispatched to the Gulf region to conduct activities such as the monitoring of cease-fire agreements as well as medical, transportation, and communications support (Hirano 1996: 36–39). The bill was accompanied by a new constitutional interpretation, promoted by Ozawa, arguing that the dispatch of SDF troops overseas under UN command was constitutional, even if the mission involved the use of force.

Predictably, pacifists in the JSP and Kōmeitō, a small centrist party founded in the 1960s by the Buddhist lay organization Sōka Gakkai, joined forces with pragmatists in the LDP, such as Gotōda Masaharu and Miyazawa Kiichi, to oppose the reinterpretation. In the protracted and chaotic Diet debate that followed, the government's various spokesmen repeatedly gave contradictory and incoherent accounts of the scope of the proposed activities and their relationship to Article Nine. The CLB also refused to offer a concrete example illustrating when transporting weapons and ammunition did not constitute the use of force. In the end, the CLB director-general reasserted his organization's original position by declaring that there was "some room for doubt about the constitutionality of SDF participation in a United Nations force" (Odawara 1991: 13). Forced to withdraw the bill without a vote, Ozawa and his supporters settled for a large monetary contribution and, once hostilities ceased, the deployment of minesweepers to the Gulf (Purrington and A. K. 1992: 318–19).

Soon thereafter, however, signs of change appeared. Stung by international criticism of Japan's failure to provide troops, the Japanese public shifted to support the minesweeper deployment (Purrington 1992: 171). Picking up on popular sentiment, revisionists began to paint Article Nine as an obstacle to "international cooperation" and the cause of a significant national embarrassment. Wielding the humiliation of "checkbook diplomacy" and assisted by conservatives in the media, the revisionists attacked the pragmatists and the pacifists simultaneously and declared war on the CLB. And, for the first time, they began to win.

Shortly after the failure of the UNPCC bill, revisionists pursued new legislation to allow the SDF to participate in UN peacekeeping operations ("the PKO bill"). Ozawa was particularly active during the two Diet sessions it took to pass the bill, chairing an influential LDP ad hoc panel which issued a report arguing that a reinterpretation of Article Nine was sufficient to allow for SDF participation in multinational forces operating under UN command or sanction (LDP 1992: 57). In this interpretation, the SDF would be permitted to fulfill combat roles. But altering the interpretation in this way was opposed by Prime Minister Miyazawa, other pragmatists in the LDP, and the CLB. When Ozawa finally brokered an agreement on the bill with Kōmeitō and another small centrist party, the SDF's mandate saw only modest expansion. Although the passage of the PKO bill in 1992 marked the first revision of the ban on overseas dispatch in nearly 40 years, the old constraints were replaced with new ones.

the passage of the PKO bill in 1992 marked the first revision of the ban on overseas dispatch in nearly 40 years

The centerpiece of these new constraints was the Five Principles. Developed by the CLB based on their earlier interpretation that the SDF could not use force as part of a UN army, these principles require the Japanese government to withdraw its troops at the first sign of hostilities while denying the SDF the right to use force to accomplish the mission of the UN operation. The Five Principles helped gain the support of not only pragmatists in the LDP but pacifist parties in the Diet as well. The small centrist parties demanded and received further concessions, however, including Kōmeitō's call for a freeze on Peacekeeping Force (PKF) partic-ipation, which kept the SDF from performing such duties as cease-fire monitoring, weapons collection and disposal, and buffer zone patrols. In more than a decade since the enactment of the PKO Law, the SDF has participated in numerous UN operations without major incident and with full public support.

From the 1950s through the 1990s, revisionists retained their *realpoli-tik* beliefs about security. As the decade of the 1990s progressed, they began to emphasize new foreign threats, such as North Korea's missile and nuclear programs, to justify a more muscular defense posture. They con-tinued to seek to upgrade Japan's position in the U.S.-Japan alliance to that of an equal partner. Accordingly a central item on their agenda remained changing Article Nine to allow for exercise of the right of col-lective self-defense.[43]

Over the decades, revisionists reproduced themselves in a variety of ways. First, as noted earlier, their numbers include several second- and third-generation politicians who have adopted constitutional positions similar to those of their fathers and grandfathers.[44] Second, they leveraged intraparty institutions such as the party platform and committee system to keep revisionist senti-ment alive.[45] They also established civic action groups and developed ties with academics and journalists who support their views.[46] Both these intraparty and extraparty activities have pro-

revisionists entered the post-Cold War period well positioned to renew the assault on Article Nine

duced reports and proposals that placed revisionist views in the public domain.[47] Finally, they repeatedly attacked security policies associated with Article Nine, such as Nakasone's successful attempt to breach the 1 per-cent of GNP ceiling on defense spending (Pyle 1987: 266–68). All things considered, revisionists entered the post-Cold War period well positioned to renew the assault on Article Nine.

After their initial Gulf War victory, by contrast, pacifists and pragma-tists limped through the 1990s. Pacifists were particularly hard hit. Leftist parties were unable to redefine themselves in the post-Cold War era and have been decimated. Instructive in this regard is the experience of the JSP, now called the Social Democratic Party of Japan (SDPJ). As centrist parties, such as Kōmeitō, began to accept the nonaggression view of Article Nine during the 1970s in order to facilitate cooperation with the governing LDP, the JSP had struggled to maintain its commitment to state nonviolence (Keddell 1993: 31–77). Thus when JSP Chairman Murayama Tomiichi declared his party's support for the U.S.-Japan alliance and the constitutionality of the SDF in 1994 (as part of a deal to form a coalition government with the LDP), some commentators declared pacifism as a political ideal "gone with the wind."[48] Adding insult to injury, this key policy shift came in the midst of a series of spectacular electoral defeats that reduced the socialists' lower house contingent from 136 seats in 1990 to a mere 6 in 2003.

Still, shifting positions and weakened Diet numbers have not completely neutralized pacifists in the Article Nine debate. In the years since 1994, the socialists have continued to emphasize the *heiwa kokka* identity in their rhetoric, and a connection between rhetoric and policy positions has remained.[49] Despite dropping their constitutional objections to the SDF and the U.S.-Japan alliance, the socialists have shifted their security policies only slightly. Their new defense program calls for the reduction and decentralization of the SDF, the establishment of a regional security organization, and the eventual transformation of the U.S.-Japan alliance to a nonmilitary relationship. In addition, the party has refocused its defense of Article Nine to oppose change in the 1954 interpretation. Kōmeitō's conversion may be viewed in a similar light. Prompted by the strong pacifist sentiments of Sōka Gakkai, the Kōmeitō platform calls for the literal realization of a "peace nation" and asserts that Japan has a historic mission to spread peace throughout the world.[50] Thus both Kōmeitō and the socialists appear to have relinquished their claim of de jure state pacifism in exchange for the potential to preserve de facto state pacifism in the policy trenches.[51] Those who used to mock the 1954 interpretation have now become its strongest defenders.

There are other reasons why pacifism cannot be completely dismissed. First, a group of former socialists and Kōmeitō members have formed a pacifist block within the Democratic Party of Japan, the largest opposition party. Under the leadership of former socialist Yokomichi Takahiro, the group has continued to emphasize "peace nation" rhetoric even in the midst of a party that has grown increasingly hawkish in its orientation.⁵² Second, while representing a significantly smaller portion of the Diet than in past decades, pacifist parties and factions (SDPJ, JCP, Kōmeitō, and Yokomichi's DPJ) still combine to hold about a sixth of the seats in the House of Representatives and nearly a quarter of the seats in the House of Councilors.⁵³ Finally, and most important, paci-fists' embrace of the 1954 interpretation has *pacifism cannot be com-pletely dismissed* made them acceptable coalition partners for the LDP. As first the social-ists and then Kōmeitō formed coalition governments with the LDP, they came closer to the seat of power than at any time since the late 1940s. As we shall see, this achievement has helped them constrain revisionism within the LDP and compensate somewhat for their declining numbers in the Diet.

During the Cold War, pragmatists reproduced themselves through factional ties and government institutions. Yoshida's influence ensured that his beliefs about security, as well as his assessment of the usefulness of Article Nine, were passed on to a cadre of younger factional leaders includ-ing future prime ministers Ikeda Hayato and Satō Eisaku. Accordingly, as key players in government during the early postwar period, pragmatists were able to institutionalize their constitutional ideas in government prac-tice.⁵⁴ In addition, pragmatists found support from the CLB, which, driv-en by institutional incentives, continued to constrain the reinterpretation schemes of revisionists.⁵⁵ Finally, like revisionists, pragmatists had some success establishing ties with academics through research institutes.⁵⁶

Despite this record of success, by the late 1990s the political ground had begun to shift beneath the pragmatists' feet. In 1998, Katō Kōichi, leader of the largest pragmatist faction in the LDP (the former Miyazawa faction), staged a rebellion against the party leadership. When it failed, the resulting fiasco led to the breakup of his faction and a significant reduction in the organized power of pragmatists within the LDP. Although pragmatists from other factions, such as Nonaka Hiromu, would remain prominent in the party hierarchy for a few more years, the flameout of the Katō faction would prove a harbinger of things to come for the pragmatists.

The three years following the passage of the PKO bill saw dramatic changes in both the international and domestic political environments. Internationally, the crisis over North Korea's nuclear program in 1994–95 forced U.S.-Japan alliance managers to focus on a new regional security problem. The escalation of tensions in the Taiwan Straits in 1996 brought back memories of 1958. Domestically, the LDP lost power for the first time in 38 years when Ozawa and others led defectors out of the party and were rewarded by voters in the July 1993 election. What followed were years of coalition governments that combined revisionists, pragmatists, and pacifists in awkward, if not quite haphazard, ways (Ōtake 2000).

The next challenge to Article Nine came from familiar quarters. Pressure from Washington—combined with agitation from LDP revisionists, the Japan Defense Agency, and the Ministry of Foreign Affairs (MOFA)—yielded the 1995 National Defense Program Outline (NDPO), which called for Japan to ensure smooth implementation of U.S.-Japan security arrangements in the event of a situation in the "areas surrounding Japan" that might affect Japan's security (*shūhen jitai*). Unsatisfied with this accomplishment, revisionists, now split between the LDP and Ozawa's New Frontier Party (NFP), pushed the JSP-LDP coalition government to reinterpret Article Nine in order to allow for collective self-defense (Mochizuki 1997: 13–14). But pragmatists such as Kōno Yōhei and Katō Kōichi, who opposed any changes to Article Nine, dominated the LDP leadership at this time. As a result of these divisions, the new guidelines governing the U.S.-Japan alliance (released in September 1997) committed Japan to provide only "rear area support" (*kōhō chiiki shien*) for U.S. forces in the event of a regional emergency involving Japan's security.

To enact changes required by the new guidelines, the LDP introduced three related bills to the Diet in 1998. Now led by Prime Minister Obuchi Keizō, the LDP formed a coalition government with Ozawa's tiny Liberal Party (LP) but required cooperation from Kōmeitō in order to get bills through the upper house. Internally the LDP was divided into four major factions; the Miyazawa and Nakasone factions represented the clearest division between pragmatists and revisionists. Behind the scenes, the prime mover in the Obuchi government, Chief Cabinet Secretary Nonaka Hiromu, scrambled to manage Diet business while trying to build a stable coalition government. A member of Obuchi's leading faction, Nonaka advocated pragmatist policies and was a close ally of Katō Kōichi, who would soon succeed Miyazawa as leader of the largest pragmatist faction. The legislation, drafted under standard CLB oversight, centered on the bill concerning "situations in areas surrounding Japan," which allowed the SDF to provide "rear area support" to U.S. forces in Japan and the surrounding areas in the event of a military emergency likely to affect Japan's security. The new SDF roles included the provision of water, food, and fuel; the transport of material (with the exception of weapons and ammunition); and medical support. In accordance with the CLB's interpretation of the ban on collective self-defense, the SDF was not allowed to use force to accomplish the goals of these missions. Although a further step away from the ban on overseas dispatch, the bill fell far short of satisfying revisionist demands for collective self-defense.[57]

The bills passed the Diet in May 1999 on the strength of the combined votes of the LDP, LP, and Kōmeitō. For its votes, Kōmeitō was able to get a provision requiring ex ante Diet approval for troop deployments, with the exception of emergencies, when ex post approval would be required. Although the party's position created tensions with its pacifist Sōka Gakkai supporters, Kōmeitō's cooperation on the bill was part of a larger plan to arrange electoral cooperation with the LDP before the next lower house election. When explaining the bill to the public, Kōmeitō leaders took pains to present it as a peace-promoting initiative designed to "prevent armed conflicts."[58] Having established an important precedent for cooperating with the LDP on a difficult issue, Kōmeitō then elected to join its erstwhile conservative opponents in a ruling government. As we shall see, the continued presence of *Kōmeitō* in the government has served as a brake on the revisionist agenda.

Despite a separation of decades, the three groups that divided politics in the 1950s managed to remain relevant in the Article Nine debate of the 1990s. With the LDP lacking a majority in the upper house, support from pacifists proved necessary to pass even normal legislation, let alone constitutional amendments. In this regard, pacifists achieved a measure of parliamentary power they could only long for in the 1950s. Further, LDP pragmatists who held important faction, party, and government posts during this period also contributed to the blocking of Ozawa's reinterpretation attempt during debate over the UNPCC bill.

The debate over Article Nine in the 1990s, however, differed from that of the 1950s in important ways. First, while pacifism as an organized political force declined in the Diet, the LDP continually failed to recapture its previous level of one-party dominance. Second, pacifists reframed their policy goals in more palatable terms. Although continuing to promote the "peace nation" identity and seeking to constrain security policy, they accepted the need to work with other players in order to influence policy and adjusted their constitutional demands accordingly. The combination of these factors encouraged a level of overt cooperation between pragmatists and pacifists that was not possible in the ideologically divided 1950s. It should thus be no surprise that on both occasions when the LDP invited a pacifist party to join a coalition government, the negotiations were supervised by pragmatists such as Kōno Yōhei, Katō Kōichi, and Nonaka Hiromu (Curtis 1999). Able to coordinate on security issues in a manner not possible in Yoshida's time, pragmatists and pacifists combined their strengths effectively to oppose major changes to Article Nine, especially the recognition of collective self-defense. From this perspective, the numerical decline among pacifists was somewhat compensated for by this new commitment to coalition politics.

pragmatists and pacifists combined their strengths effectively to oppose major changes to Article Nine

Still, revisionists secured several major legislative victories in the 1990s, including the establishment of Diet constitutional research commissions that issued their final reports in April 2005. They were also joined by influential new allies in the media and academia. The *Yomiuri Shimbun,* Japan's largest daily newspaper, has become a staunch advocate of constitutional reform, including allowing exercise of the right of collective self-defense. While Japanese universities continue to produce and employ academics advocating pacifist positions, the new generation includes more scholars in favor of changing Article Nine than was the case in the 1950s.[59] By the end of the decade, revisionist support and accomplishments had begun to pile up. The Self-Defense Force was able to engage in a growing list of widely accepted activities that once had been deemed unconstitutional. And now the future of Article Nine itself was far from certain.

Still, revisionists secured several major legislative victories in the 1990s

Koizumi's Challenge

Polls of Diet members in recent years have shown growing support for constitutional revision in general and for amending Article Nine in particular. In 2002, the *Yomiuri Shimbun* found that 71 percent of Diet members favored revising the constitution, an increase of 11 points from its

1997 poll. With regard to Article Nine, the same *Yomiuri* poll noted that 55 percent of Diet members favored revision, up 14 points from the previous survey. On the central question of whether Japan should be allowed to exercise the right to collective self-defense, 54 percent agreed while 40 percent opposed.[60]

What explains the tremendous rise of revisionist sentiment in the Diet? Although many factors—including shifts in the regional balance of power—are in play in the constitutional debate, we continue to find it useful to focus on the enduring tripartite division among domestic forces. We trace the rise of revisionism primarily to three factors: the failure of leftist parties to redefine themselves in a shifted political landscape; national and party-level institutional reforms that have strengthened the role of the prime minister within the LDP

What explains the tremendous rise of revisionist sentiment in the Diet?

and in the policymaking process; and the leadership of the current prime minister, Koizumi Junichirō. In short, changes in partisanship, institutions, and leadership have been critical drivers behind the rise of revisionism over the last decade. We now consider each in turn.

Why have leftist parties populated largely by pacifists suffered such significant electoral defeats over the last decade? Surely this question requires a complex answer. Perhaps the simplest explanation is that the collapse of the Soviet Union in 1991 served in some general way to discredit the left in the minds of Japanese voters. We disagree with this interpretation. For one thing, the Japan Communist Party, certainly the organization most identified with international communism, actually gained seats in the Diet for years after the collapse of the Soviet Union before suffering major defeats in the last few election cycles. Moreover, leftist parties in other democracies, such as the Communist Party of Italy or the Labor Party in Britain, were able to reinvent themselves successfully in the post-Cold War era.[61] This development undermines the assertion that the end of the Cold War spelled doom for leftist parties around the globe.

Nor was the decline of the old left a direct result of the parties' positions on Article Nine. Although the socialists unceremoniously discarded their signature stance on the constitution while the communists stubbornly clung to theirs, the results have been the same. The SDPJ and the JCP currently hold only eleven and eighteen seats, respectively, in the

Diet. In our view this decline stemmed primarily from leadership failures. For example, the seeds of the socialists' collapse were sown long before the end of the Cold War, when their leadership failed to defend the party's organizational base in the public-sector unions from Nakasone's administrative reform drive.[62] When these reforms precipitated the 1989 collapse of Sōhyō (General Council of Trade Unions in Japan), the largest public-sector union, the socialists' long kiss goodnight was already well along. As international ideological divisions eased following the collapse of the Soviet Union, leaders of the SDPJ and JCP repeatedly failed to seize the opportunity to redefine themselves despite the availability of successful models of "third way" politics from Britain, the United States, Italy, and elsewhere. The final nail in the SDPJ coffin—Murayama's disastrous decision to join the LDP in a coalition government in 1994—is a prime example of this failure. When the JSP joined its erstwhile enemy in government without a strategy for maintaining its distinctiveness in the minds of voters, the party's demoralized base as well as nonaffiliated voters naturally looked elsewhere for an alternative to the LDP's conservative policies. The communists, too, have so far proved unable to hold onto nonaffiliated (sometimes called "floating") voters. In particular, their leaders' refusal to moderate long-held ideological positions has kept them from cooperating with other opposition parties and relegated them to the margins of national politics.[63]

The flip side of the decline of pacifist parties has been the rise of the LDP as a genuinely revisionist party. We see this as a consequence of two related factors. First, a series of institutional reforms has strengthened the LDP party leadership—especially the power of the prime minister and party president—at the expense of factional leaders and other power centers both inside and outside the party. And second, the current party leadership, led by Prime Minister Koizumi, is the most popular group of revisionists ever to have held power. There have been revisionist cabinets in the past, of course, but neither Kishi Nobusuke, Fukuda Takeo, Nakasone Yasuhiro, nor any other revisionist prime minister had ever enjoyed Koizumi's degree of centralized power or popular support. And Koizumi has directed his strongly revisionist leadership on a course that has pushed Article Nine to the political front burner for the first time in 50 years.

The institutional changes in question include electoral and campaign finance reforms, changes in the LDP presidential election process, as well as several other government and administrative reforms. Although it is still too early to know the full impact of these changes, it seems clear that one of their cumulative effects has been to strengthen the power of the LDP leadership, particularly the party president and prime minister. The 1994 electoral reforms, for example, which replaced Japan's infamous multi-member, single nontransferable vote (SNTV) districts with a combination of single-seat and proportional representation (PR) districts, reduced intraparty competition among LDP candidates and thus their dependence on factional support to get nominated to contest a specific district. Some have even argued that factional influence is no longer salient in the nomination process for either single-seat or PR districts (Cox et al. 1999: 42–43). Moreover, campaign finance reforms increased party leaders' control of the distribution of funds to party candidates. Although factional leaders had reduced their fund-raising activities beginning in the 1970s, new regulations banning political donations to groups other than the parties themselves have further strengthened the party leadership's role in campaign finance (Krauss and Pekkanen 2004: 15).

The diffusion of factional divisions within the LDP is particularly relevant to the question of Article Nine. As factional leaders jostled for power within the LDP, they often used positions on constitutional reform to differentiate themselves, leaving the party unable to unify on a common revision position (Fukui 1970). In particular, mainstream factional leaders advocated the retention of Article Nine while anti-mainstream leaders sought revision. Even with the emergence of the enormous Tanaka faction in the 1970s, a relative balance was maintained among pro- and anti-Article Nine factions and the resulting internal division precluded serious attempts to revise the peace clause. As these recent reforms have weakened the power of factional leaders, their role in maintaining the constitutional status quo within the party has also declined.

The 2001 reform of the LDP presidential election process can be seen as both a consequence and a further deepening of the decline in factional power. Angered by the lack of transparency that accompanied the selection of faction leader Mori Yoshirō to replace Obuchi Keizō following his sudden death in 2000, younger LDP Diet members demanded that the party presidential election process be opened to local party members. Although faction leaders managed to reduce the weight of votes from outside the Diet in the system eventually adopted, its first implementation resulted in the election of Koizumi over his nearest rival, the leader of the largest faction at that time, Hashimoto Ryūtarō. This surprising result made

Koizumi the "first LDP president and prime minister to be selected out-side the traditional factional power struggles" (Shinoda 2003: 23). If this procedure continues to be followed, it means that future party leaders will have to reach beyond the factional balance in the Diet to appeal to local party leaders, thus further reducing the influence of faction leaders.

Finally, a series of government and administrative reforms passed dur-ing the late 1990s has increased the role of the prime minister and the cab-inet in the policymaking process. The first set of measures was demanded by Ozawa Ichirō when he brought his now defunct Liberal Party into a coalition government with the LDP in 1999. They included a reduction in the size of the cabinet and limitations on the Diet testimony of bureau-crats, both designed to streamline cabinet decision making and reduce the influence of bureaucrats in policymaking (Shinoda 2003). The second set of measures was part of a broad-based administrative reform effort initiat-ed by the Hashimoto administration in 1998, although some changes were not implemented until 2001. These included a revision of the Cabinet Law, which clarified the prime minister's authority to introduce policy ini-tiatives and strengthened the ability of cabinet members to take action without first obtaining the approval of the relevant government bureau-cracy. The Hashimoto reforms also rationalized the Cabinet Secretariat by merging three policy offices into one to reduce coordination problems and creating a director of crisis management. The result has been a more flex-ible apparatus capable of forming offices on ad hoc issues and reducing government response time during crises (Schoff 2004: 82–90).

These changes are important to the Article Nine debate because they have helped the Koizumi administration push the envelope of interpreta-tion in crafting his responses to the September 11 attacks on the United States and the 2003 Iraq War. It should also be noted that these changes were initiated and pushed to realization by revisionists such as Ozawa and Hashimoto. Although their views on Article Nine, particularly their dis-may that constitutional interpretations hampered Japan's response to the first Gulf War, were likely animating factors in their desire to increase the power and effectiveness of the prime minister's office, Article Nine was clearly only one issue among many. For example, Ozawa, an early oppo-nent of the multimember district electoral system, supported electoral reform primarily as part of a broad plan to introduce a two-party system, which he believed was more effective at governing. Although, as the author of the UNPCC bill, Ozawa was no doubt particularly angry at Kaifu's failure to dispatch the SDF in 1990, he had developed his electoral reform plan long before Iraq invaded Kuwait (Samuels 2003a: 328). Moreover, the overwhelmingly negative view of the Murayama government's response to the Great Hanshin Earthquake in 1995 was another major factor in the drive to improve crisis management institutions and helped put strengthening the power of the prime minister's office on the agenda in the Hashimoto administration (Shinoda 2003: 25). It is thus impossible to attribute the motivations behind these reforms solely to the demands of security policy or the desire to revise Article Nine.

Perhaps even more important, these institutional changes have been accompanied by the rise of party leaders willing to leverage the new power they provide. In particular, Prime Minister Koizumi has repeatedly refused to assign cabinet appointments on the basis of factional affiliations. Although these reforms have not ended the power of factions, they have weakened them.[64] In the 2003 lower house election, the majority of new candidates ran without factional affiliation, and today almost 10 percent of current LDP Diet members have no factional affiliation.

Koizumi's exercise of these new levers of party power has not been limited to the apportionment of cabinet posts. He has also used this power to strengthen his support base within the party. Before becoming prime minister, Koizumi was a member of the faction led by former Prime Minister Mori Yoshirō, and his support remains concentrated there. Although he has since renounced this factional affiliation, Koizumi has used his control of the party leadership to favor his old colleagues. Over the last two years, the LDP has contested elections in both houses of the Diet. Despite disappointing performances for the party on both occasions, factions supportive of Koizumi's leadership and policies picked up seats while those in opposition lost seats. Of particular note was the strong performance of the Mori faction, the only major faction to pick up seats in both elections. Koizumi's intraparty opponents, concentrated in the Hashimoto and Kamei factions, suffered mightily, losing seats in both elections. In the end, the Mori faction reached near parity with the Hashimoto faction (formerly the Tanaka faction) for the first time since this group was put together by former Prime Minister Tanaka Kakuei in the 1970s. Following that lower house election, Kamei Shizuka, leader of the Kamei faction, wondered out loud to reporters if Koizumi had dissolved the Diet for the sole purpose of gaining seats for the Mori faction.[65] The Mori faction's continued success under Koizumi's leadership also produced grumbling from the other factions following the party's poor performance in the upper house election.[66]

A side effect of this power play has been the consolidation of party power in the hands of revisionists. And who are they today? They are direct heirs of the traditional revisionist line—literally the sons and grandsons of Kishi Nobusuke and his closest allies. Prime Minister Koizumi is the scion of a distinguished line of the anti-mainstream revisionists whose efforts to revise the constitution had been thoroughly frustrated. The prime minister's father, Junya, became defense minister in the early 1960s and Junichirō's first job in politics was as an aide to one of his father's like-minded colleagues and a future prime minister, Fukuda Takeo. It is no mere coincidence, then, that on winning the premiership Koizumi appointed Kishi's grandson, Abe Shinzō, as deputy chief cabinet secretary (and later LDP secretary-general) and Fukuda's son, Fukuda Yasuo, as chief cabinet secretary. While by no means a carbon copy of his father, Prime Minister Koizumi is the most pro-revision prime minister in four decades. This was apparent right from the beginning when he became the first prime minister since Kishi to refuse to endorse the constitutional status quo when he took office in April 2001. He has also given vocal support to revisionists on numerous occasions—including publicly toying with the idea of reinterpreting Article Nine to allow for collective self-defense.[67] And as we shall see, he has pushed policies that have taken Japan right up to the edge of the 1954 interpretation and, some say, beyond.

[the revisionists today] are direct heirs of the traditional revisionist line

Koizumi is the most pro-revision prime minister in four decades

Two trends are apparent as this wedding of revisionist ambition with stronger leadership affects the constitutional debate. First, support for constitutional revision within the LDP has grown both in scale and scope under Koizumi's leadership. In a 1997 *Yomiuri* poll of Diet members, just more than half of the LDP favored revising Article Nine. In 2002, nearly nine in ten LDP parliamentarians were in favor of revision—and allowing Japan to exercise the right of collective self-defense.[68] Second, as Koizumi has increased his control during the LDP over the last three years, pragmatists have increasingly lost out to revisionists within the party. Examples are numerous. In 2002, Katō Kōichi was forced to resign his Diet seat in a scandal. A year later, Koizumi forced the retirement of Miyazawa Kiichi, the arch-pragmatist and Yoshida disciple. Finally, just prior to the 2003 lower house election, Nonaka Hiromu, who had almost single-handedly carried the pragmatist agenda through the Obuchi and Mori administrations, announced his retirement from the Diet after expressing frustration at the increasing power of the revisionist party leadership. Although Katō has since been reelected, he and other prominent pragmatists, such as Kōno Yōhei and Koga Makoto, are weaker than ever in party councils. The consolidation of party power behind revisionist leadership has thus worked to marginalize pragmatists and unify the LDP around revisionist goals to an unprecedented degree.

As these internal changes were occurring within the LDP, external events provided revisionists with further opportunities to challenge the constitutional status quo. Following the September 2001 terrorist attacks on New York and Washington, Prime Minister Koizumi took advantage of his newly improved institutional and political position to craft a response that surprised observers with both its speed and the degree to which it pushed the envelope of constitutional interpretation. One week after the attacks, Koizumi announced a seven-point plan featuring a clear pledge to dispatch the SDF to assist U.S. operations against Taliban and Al Qaeda forces.[69] Legislation enacting this plan (the Antiterrorism Law) passed the lower house less than one month later and became law before the end of October. Among several other measures, the final law allowed the dispatch of MSDF ships to the Indian Ocean to engage in medical, transportation, and refueling activities in support of U.S. forces fighting in Afghanistan. In comparison with the long and difficult deliberations that ended in the failure of the UNPCC bill, the speed and scope of this accomplishment are astonishing. They become more understandable, however, when one considers how the institutional and political changes described here combined to provide Koizumi with levers of power that were not available to past prime ministers.

First, Koizumi was able to use the expanded crisis management capabilities of the cabinet office to develop an initial response plan without relying excessively on outside ministries or LDP party councils. In the early hours after the attack, Koizumi made use of the Cabinet Crisis Management Center to coordinate his initial response and soon declared the situation a "serious emergency," placing Chief Cabinet Secretary Fukuda Yasuo in charge of managing related operations. Following a meeting of the National Security Council the next morning, Koizumi took advantage of his expanded ability to establish ad hoc offices by assigning Deputy Chief Cabinet Secretary Furukawa Teijirō to establish a task force to craft a response plan. In addition to members of the cabinet office, the task force included selected senior officials from MOFA, JDA, and the CLB. Furukawa also reassigned an existing Cabinet Secretariat study group, originally created to consider emergency legislation, to provide the technical expertise necessary to mold the task force's decisions into draft policies.[70] In this way, by centralizing policymaking within the Cabinet Secretariat, Koizumi was able to reduce interministerial conflict and speed up the policymaking process. When a disagreement arose between MOFA and the JDA over whether the SDF dispatch could be justified under the existing guidelines, Koizumi was able to intervene decisively by ordering the task force to draft new ad hoc legislation (Hughes 2002: 12–14). Thus a major conflict was avoided and the process was entirely contained within the Cabinet Secretariat.

Second, and perhaps more surprising, Koizumi was able to formulate his initial plans without major consultations with his own party. Although he consulted with LDP Secretary-General Yamasaki Taku early in the process, this relationship was far different from the one that existed between Prime Minister Kaifu and Secretary-General Ozawa during the UNPCC debacle. In addition to his party position, Ozawa had also been deputy head of the largest faction in the LDP at the time, whereas Kaifu was from a small faction and thus needed Ozawa's support to get his policies through the party. Koizumi, by contrast, had ignored factional affiliation in his cabinet and party appointments: Yamasaki, although the leader of a small faction, was better known as a close political ally of Koizumi. Unlike Kaifu, Koizumi was also confident that his extremely high public approval rating could be leveraged in pushing his plan through the LDP party councils (Shinoda 2003: 30). The shift in the power balance between the prime minister and his party is clear from the sequence of the policy process. Before Koizumi presented his plan to the LDP General Council on September 27, he had already held a press conference to announce its main points, reached an agreement with his partners in the governing coalition, and even briefed the opposition parties. The policy thus arrived on the General Council's doorstep largely as a fait accompli.

And although Koizumi ended up making important concessions to Kōmeitō—including inserting a two-year sunset provision, banning the transport of weapons, and requiring Diet approval for the deployment plan—he made only minor compromises that can be directly traced to demands emanating from within his own party. Chief among these was the decision not to send destroyers equipped with the advanced Aegis fire control system.[71] This move was opposed by pragmatists such as Nonaka Hiromu and Katō Kōichi, who saw it as unnecessarily provocative to regional neighbors and worried that the ships' ability to share target information with U.S. forces might lead to a violation of the ban on collective self-defense (Hughes 2002: 17–20). Finally, Koizumi also demonstrated his control over his own cabinet by submitting the bill to the Diet from the Cabinet Secretariat rather than the Ministry of Foreign Affairs, which would normally handle Diet deliberations in this area. He was thus able to assign the role of guiding the bill through the Diet to Chief Cabinet Secretary Fukuda rather than the popular but eccentric Foreign Minister Tanaka Makiko, whom he was not confident could effectively handle questions on the bill (Shinoda 2004: 60).

Although the Antiterrorism Law applied constitutional logic similar to that in the guidelines and PKO laws, the MSDF deployment was authorized in a situation when Japan's security was not directly threatened and outside the auspices of a relevant UN peacekeeping operation. Its constitutional justification combined something old with something new. First, the government stressed the fact that the use of force was not sanctioned to accomplish the mission—thus placing the deployment outside the constraints of Article Nine, as was the case with "rear area support" in the guidelines legislation (Hughes 2002: 20–21). Second, since the United States had justified its attack on Afghanistan on self-defense grounds, MSDF support for U.S. operations would seem to violate the ban on collective self-defense. Here the Koizumi administration justified the deployment as a noncombat, collective security operation in accordance with both the preamble of Japan's constitution, which urges Japan "to strive for the preservation of peace," and UN Resolution 1368, which urges member nations to cooperate against terrorist threats to international security (Shinoda 2003: 31; Hughes 2002: 21–23). This reasoning, which echoed ideas offered by an LDP committee chaired by Ozawa in 1992, opened a new avenue for SDF dispatch while retaining the central constraint on the use of force.[72] In the end, the bill passed swiftly through the Diet and the

SDF was dispatched to the Indian Ocean with the mandate to provide fuel but little else to U.S. and British forces. Clearly the operation fell far short of some revisionists' hopes (Heginbotham and Samuels 2002b: 102).

Although the pragmatists and pacifists were again able to constrain revisionists somewhat on this occasion, their ability to leverage each other's strength into significant revisionist concessions was on the decline. This became apparent as Japan faced its next major external challenge: the U.S.-led invasion of Iraq in 2003. At first, Japan's response seemed consistent with the pragmatist-pacifist line. Although the Koizumi government offered diplomatic support for the United States in the face of domestic opposition, it refused to join the wartime operations of the "coalition of the willing." Moreover, Koizumi cited Article Nine as the reason why Japan could not provide combat troops. Following the end of major military operations, however, revisionists began to push hard to send the SDF to Iraq as part of Japan's contribution to the reconstruction effort. As was the case with the Antiterrorism Law, Koizumi again leveraged his institutional and political position to craft an Iraq policy that challenged Article Nine's constraints more than ever before. This case is even more extraordinary when one considers that Koizumi's popularity had declined considerably by this time (partly as a consequence of his Iraq War stance) and the public was largely opposed to deploying the SDF in postwar Iraq.[73] Despite facing new obstacles, Koizumi turned to the same methods he had employed to pass the Antiterrorism Law. To the surprise of some, they again produced results.

The first maneuver Koizumi reprised was the establishment of an ad hoc office within the Cabinet Secretariat to coordinate Iraq policy. Within this Iraq Response Team (Iraku Mondai Taisaku Honbu), which Koizumi headed, a small group under Assistant Cabinet Secretary Ōmori Keiji was formed to develop a new law should an SDF deployment be pursued.[74] By the beginning of April, the group issued the opinion that existing UN resolutions were not sufficient justification to conduct an SDF deployment under the PKO Law: a new law would be necessary to enable an Iraq operation. By early June, the group proposed that the new law should use existing UN resolutions (such as UN Resolution 1483) as the legal basis for action, should restrict operations to "noncombat zones" (*hisentōchiiki*), and should avoid reviewing the use-of-force restrictions already in place in order to ensure swift enactment (Shinoda 2004: 105).

The second technique Koizumi again employed skillfully was in sequencing the rollout of his plan in such a way as to reduce the influence of the LDP policy councils. Once the bill's framework had been determined, Koizumi and Fukuda first met with the secretary-generals of the governing coalition parties to notify them of the government's intention to introduce the bill to the Diet. It was agreed at this meeting to add a four-year sunset clause to the bill. Koizumi also asked for the cooperation of the governing parties at a meeting of the government/ruling party liaison conference (*seifu yotō renraku kaigi*). The representatives of the Cabinet Secretariat team then explained the bill (the Iraq Reconstruction Law) to a joint session of two committees established between the LDP and Kōmeitō to discuss Iraq, North Korea, and terrorism issues.[75] Only after all this did the team present the bill to the relevant subcommittees of the LDP Policy Affairs Research Council (PARC) on June 10. After three days of deliberations, a compromise was reached to leave the definition of "non-combat zone" out of the bill. When the bill was subsequently presented to the LDP General Affairs Council, pragmatists such as Nonaka again fought to curtail its scope—this time successfully removing provisions authorizing SDF participation in the disposal of weapons of mass destruction materials. The bill then received cabinet approval on June 16.[76] Although the bill was opposed by all opposition parties—and some prominent pragmatists, including Nonaka and Koga Makoto, abstained in the lower house vote—it passed both houses of the Diet and became law before the end of July.[77]

The speed with which this legislation was realized again bears comment. It took only two months from Koizumi's first public reference to the possibility of sending the SDF on May 21 to the passage of the Iraq Reconstruction Law on July 26. Keeping debate to a minimum, Koizumi and his allies had again pushed a bill through the Diet authorizing an SDF deployment. Facing a lower house election in November and growing violence on the ground in Iraq, however, Koizumi delayed the deployment plan for months. His cabinet finally approved an action plan in mid-December, and deployment of a 1,000-man force was completed in spring 2004. Japanese forces have now been in Samawah for over a year and have already seen their tour of duty extended by the Diet

> *it is hard to understand [Japan's Iraq policy] as anything short of a turning point*

once. Whereas other U.S. allies have come to Iraq, shown the flag, and departed, the SDF has stayed for the duration. With armed Japanese troops remaining on the ground in a hostile environment and with the Koizumi government implementing a kind of de facto collective self-defense, it is hard to understand this as anything short of a turning point in Japan's postwar security policy.

In developing and implementing Japan's Iraq policy, Koizumi and his revisionist allies took actions that at first reaffirmed and then ignored Article Nine. During the lead-up to the Iraq War, the Koizumi administration cited Article Nine to justify Japan's refusal to send combat troops. Following the end of major hostilities, however, Koizumi and JDA head Ishiba Shigeru pushed hard for a human contribution to the postwar reconstruction, emphasizing the ineffectiveness of Japan's "checkbook diplomacy" during the first Gulf War. Although their plan included an SDF deployment, they argued it was consistent with Article Nine since the troops would not be allowed to use force to accomplish their mission and Iraq was no longer a "combat zone" (*sentōchiiki*). But as the security situation in Iraq deteriorated during the late summer and fall of 2003, this second assertion became increasingly problematic. Nonetheless, despite the admission by both the United States military and Japanese survey missions that an armed insurgency was under way, Koizumi continued to argue that Article Nine's prohibitions were not relevant to the planned SDF mission. On the day he announced cabinet approval of the deployment, Koizumi avoided mention of Article Nine at all. This strategy seemed designed to avoid legal and political complications. On the legal side, Koizumi's claim not to be challenging past interpretations of Article Nine allowed him to avoid further legalistic wrangling with the CLB. Politically this strategy seemed aimed at maintaining support for the deployment among advocates of Article Nine in the governing coalition, including the Kōmeitō and LDP pragmatists, who had begun to express doubts about the SDF's mission. In addition, ignoring the policy's Article Nine implications also reduced the ability of the DPJ, which opposed the deployment, to exploit the constitutional issue. Whether this strategy will work in the long run remains to be seen, but it has produced a glaring inconsistency between the government's protestations of support for past Article Nine interpretations and its actual policy initiatives.

Considering these developments, one must wonder how Article Nine has so far survived the Koizumi administration. The answer again lies in the shifting institutional bases of the revisionists, pragmatists, and pacifists—this time the presence of Kōmeitō in the ruling coalition. Thus the weakened pragmatists have been able to leverage the pacifist vote in coalition councils and moderate revisionist demands. In this way, the numerical decline among pacifists and pragmatists has been somewhat compensated for by the requirements of coalition politics. This is one reason why Article Nine remained on the books. But another factor was also at work. Over the last fifteen years, Article Nine has been used by pragmatists and revisionists alike to keep Japan from contributing combat forces to the Gulf War, the Afghanistan conflict, and even hypothetical contingencies in surrounding areas that might impact upon Japan's own security. Indeed, Article Nine was invoked by Koizumi himself when, faced with an uncertain economy and a militarily assertive alliance partner, he refused to contribute combat forces for the invasion of Iraq. Although Japan eventually did deploy the SDF on a humanitarian mission, combat remains off the table. This stance was affirmed when Chief Cabinet Secretary Hosoda Hiroyuki mused publicly that the outbreak of violence in Samawah could lead to the withdrawal of Japanese forces.[78] The lesson here is that one should never underestimate the value of Article Nine as a tool of alliance management.

Despite continuing to play the Article Nine card, revisionists remain publicly committed to realizing formal change in the future and have developed strategies to avoid bureaucratic and political resistance to informal change as well. The balance of power within the conservative majority is shifting at last. The LDP is now headed by revisionist leaders who openly champion a stronger posture for Japan in international affairs, and the party is becoming more unified on key issues in the constitutional debate, including revising Article Nine. Five decades of tripartite political dynamics among pacifists, revisionists, and pragmatists may finally be changing in ways that alter the dynamics of constitutional politics that protected Article Nine so well.

The central obstacle to change, the pragmatist/pacifist coalition, has been greatly weakened. Although pragmatists and pacifists remain on the scene, their power to keep constitutional revision from the political agenda is gone. It was this power that kept the revisionists from taking their case to the people. The major fault line of postwar politics has thus shifted. And as a result, the document that gave power to the Japanese people is now available for their reconsideration for the first time in 50 years. No matter how the current debate over Article Nine concludes, this development is itself nothing less than a turning point for Japanese democracy. Japan may not yet have become a "normal nation" with this change, but it is certainly becoming a more normal democracy.

Whither Article Nine?

Can Article Nine survive in this new environment? Recent developments give the impression that change is in the works. First, as noted earlier, revisionists are firmly in control of the LDP. Polls taken before the recent Diet elections consistently showed that nearly nine out of ten LDP candidates favored constitutional revision.[79] What is more, a poll of the candidates contesting the 2004 upper house election found that 88 percent of LDP candidates favored revising Article Nine, while 78 percent agreed that Japan should be allowed to exercise the right of collective self-defense.[80] Koizumi may have declared that constitutional revision will not happen during his tenure as prime minister, but he has set his party on an overtly revisionist trajectory. In 2004 he announced that the LDP would unveil an official constitutional revision proposal in time for the party's fiftieth anniversary in November 2005. Despite long years of revisionist agitation, the LDP has never unified behind a specific revision proposal. This will likely change when the newly established LDP New Constitution Drafting Committee (Jimintō Shinkenpō Kisō Iinkai), chaired by key Koizumi ally Mori Yoshirō, completes its work and issues a proposal to the party leadership later this year. Based on preliminary drafts made public in April and July 2005, it appears this proposal will call for revising Article Nine.[81]

There are other auspicious signs. First, opinion in the Diet has swung decisively in favor of constitutional revision. A March 2004 *Yomiuri* poll of lower house parliamentarians found that eight in ten supported formally amending the constitution.[82] Other polls have shown similar levels of Diet enthusiasm.[83] Although this does not necessarily translate into enthusiasm for changing Article Nine, it does appear to be easing the way for change in general. For example, one long-standing problem for revisionists has been the lack of formal procedures to govern the revision process.[84] Although revisionists have tried on three past occasions to enact legislation clarifying such procedures, they have never succeeded.[85] In

> *Can Article Nine survive in this new environment?*

2001, a suprapartisan group of Diet members pushing for constitutional revision prepared draft bills for these procedures, but Kōmeitō opposed moving forward on the legislation and a 2002 *Yomiuri* poll found only a plurality (49 percent) of Diet members in favor of establishing a revision procedure.[86] By 2004, however, things had changed. In March, *Yomiuri* found that nearly nine in ten lower house members approved of establishing amendment procedures.[87] The LDP developed a new draft of the bills in December 2004, and Kōmeitō agreed to drop its objections in February 2005.[88] The coalition partners are now in negotiations with the DPJ to empower the constitutional research commissions, whose original tenures expired in April 2005, with the authority to deliberate over the draft bills. Although the original goal was to have a procedure in place by June and newspaper editorialists have demanded prompt action on the matter, the LDP may push the final vote off until the end of the year or perhaps early 2006.[89] Still, for those who have waited half a century, a few more months are not likely to dampen their spirits.

Second, the DPJ and Kōmeitō have begun to show support for the revisionist project in other ways. The DPJ set up a party committee to develop its own revision proposal. The committee released an interim report in June 2004 that called for changes to Article Nine—including allowing Japan to use force in collective security operations provided an appropriate United Nations resolution is passed. Restricting Japan's use of force overseas to UN collective security operations has long been championed by Ozawa Icirō, who, following the merger of the DPJ with his Liberal Party in 2003, brought his revisionist energy and vision to the largest opposition party. The DPJ is scheduled to arrive at a final proposal by 2006. Kōmeitō, in addition to dropping its opposition to the revision procedure bills, has also signaled a willingness to support specific constitutional amendments favored by other parties, particularly the expansion of the rights of citizens. Kōmeitō support for some amendments is significant, since it creates the possibility for constitutional horse-trading in the future. The public, too, appears amenable to constitutional change. Public opinion polls taken in 2004 show that a majority of the Japanese public favors revising the constitution and that support for constitutional change has been increasing for a decade.[90]

In April 2005, the constitutional research commissions of both Diet houses released their final reports. The lower house panel produced "majority opinions" (*tasū iken*) on several issues related to Article Nine—

including specifying in the constitution the right of self-defense, the constitutional place of the SDF, and a role for the SDF in United Nations collective security operations.[91] But the commission divided three ways over the thorny issue of allowing the exercise of collective self-defense, with roughly equal numbers supporting allowing its unrestricted exercise, permitting its exercise only with restrictions, and maintaining the existing ban. In addition, those in favor of allowing collective self-defense differed over whether or not it was necessary to make explicit reference to the right in the constitution.[92] More problematic for revisionists

[the] ultimate failure to reach consensus on many... central issues...underscores the challenges still facing revisionists

was the upper house report. Although favorable to constitutional revision in some areas, such as the inclusion of new individual rights, the upper house panel was unable to reach a consensus on changes to Article Nine. In the end, the only Article Nine issue the majority in both panels agreed on was a nonchange: maintaining the first paragraph intact.[93] Pro-revision editorialists could not hide their disappointment with this mixed result.[94] Thus although the Diet commissions identified some points of agreement among the major parties, their ultimate failure to reach consensus on many of the central issues of the Article Nine debate underscores the challenges still facing revisionists.

These challenges are both institutional and political. Perhaps the most serious obstacle is the fact that the governing coalition is divided over the Article Nine question. Kōmeitō strongly supports maintaining Article Nine in its present form. The majority within the party (as expressed in its October 2004 action plan) opposes specific changes to Article Nine's two paragraphs and affirms the government interpretation that Japan cannot use force in collective self-defense.[95] Accordingly, Kōmeitō itself is a hotbed of opposition to changing Article Nine. In a 2004 poll of candidates contesting the upper house election, Kōmeitō candidates overwhelmingly opposed revising Article Nine

Kōmeitō...is a hotbed of opposition to changing Article Nine

(71 percent) *and* the notion that Japan should be able to exercise the right of collective self-defense (86 percent).[96] Party president Kanzaki Takenori has stated clearly that Kōmeitō will leave the governing coalition if the

LDP chooses to pursue constitutional changes with which his party disagrees.[97] This threat is not an idle one. Recent elections have enhanced Kōmeitō's position within the coalition. In 2004, the LDP was unable to take back a majority in the House of Councilors and thus must continue to rely on Kōmeitō to get legislation through the chamber. More important, the LDP has become highly dependent on Kōmeitō to deliver Sōka Gakkai voters to the polls in support of LDP candidates for lower house single seat constituencies. According to one analysis, the LDP would have lost 81 seats in the 2003 election in the absence of Kōmeitō support.[98] With the DPJ close on its heels in both houses of the Diet, the LDP can ill afford to alienate such a useful partner. Kōmeitō has worked hard over the past five years to moderate the LDP's revisionist ambitions, and seems likely to continue to do so.

Moreover the LDP, while united to an unprecedented degree over constitutional revision, remains divided on some of the specifics of its own Article Nine strategy. Although the LDP draft proposal leaked to the press in November 2004 argued that the right of collective self-defense should be recognized without restriction, this position is not universally held within the party. In particular, there is concern that such recognition may result in Japan being drawn by the United States into distant conflicts with little relation to Japan's national interests.[99] Yamasaki Taku, a former LDP secretary-general and staunch supporter of collective self-defense rights, gave voice to this fear in June 2002:

> [By enacting my proposal for revising Article Nine], the right of collective self-defense will become constitutionally recognized. But from a security point of view, *I wonder if it would be better to restrict the exercise of this right*, such as by limiting it to emergency contingencies in areas surrounding Japan that have a serious impact on Japan's peace and stability. *A hard-line concept, such as fighting together with the United States to the four corners of the earth, should not be adopted.*[100]

To address this concern, some have suggested that only restricted forms of collective self-defense should be allowed. One such scheme would limit Japan's exercise of collective self-defense to cases in which the United States, Japan's only military ally, is attacked by another state. Since the world's only superpower is unlikely to be challenged in this way in the near future, Article Nine so revised would maintain much of its value as a hedging instrument.[101] Other proposals would attach restrictions to the exercise of collective self-defense at the subconstitutional level, perhaps in the form of a basic defense law.[102] This would convert the debate over restrictions from a constitutional matter to normal Diet business, likely increasing flexibility in security policymaking. As the LDP prepares its revision proposal, it will have to resolve these disagreements.

And revisionists will not be able to count on Koizumi's leadership for much longer. His current term as LDP president expires in September 2006. Unless party rules are changed, he will have to step down as prime minister at that time. In addition, with his popularity rating falling below 50 percent (and reaching an all-time low of 33 percent in January 2005), Koizumi has become more vulnerable to challenges from within his own party.[103] Finally, and perhaps most importantly, he has expended enormous amounts of political capital in a bruising fight over reforming the postal savings system. The degree to which he will be able to push the constitutional revision debate forward in the twilight of his tenure is thus in question.

And, there are other hurdles. Revisionists in the LDP will have to reach out to like-minded members of the DPJ in order to achieve the necessary two-thirds majority. Koizumi has already publicly appealed for cooperation on constitutional reform from the opposition parties. The DPJ, however, may not be a suitable partner for the LDP. First, the Democrats have their own ideas about how

And, there are other hurdles

to revise the constitution in general and Article Nine in particular. As noted earlier, the June 2004 DPJ proposal for changing Article Nine required a United Nations resolution for Japan to be allowed to use force for collective security.[104] Including such a bright-line distinction in the constitution is at odds with current LDP thinking in both style and substance. Whether a compromise can be reached is not clear. Second, the DPJ cannot be expected to cooperate with the LDP without major concessions. They have slowly built up their Diet strength through electoral successes and party mergers and now stand within striking distance of becoming the ruling party. As Japanese politics has moved toward a two-party system, the calculus of compromise has shifted. With the Democrats so close to a breakthrough, they will not so easily hand the LDP a victory on an issue as prominent as constitutional revision.

Third, the Democrats are themselves split on the issue. The largest opposition party is a mixture of veteran politicians who switched parties and younger politicians who came into politics as Democrats. Among the veterans, Yokomichi's group of pacifists continues to restrain and divide the party over Article Nine.[105] In a 2004 poll of upper house candidates, DPJ members opposed revising Article Nine by a narrow margin (40 percent to 34 percent) but a solid majority (54 percent to 20 percent) opposed allowing the exercise of the right of collective self-defense.[106] In addition, the fact that the DPJ opposed the Iraq deployment on constitutional grounds suggests two possibilities: either the DPJ will continue to exploit this issue as the events of the deployment unfold—a strategy that would further complicate cooperation with the LDP on Article Nine revision—or it will split. Indeed, we should not be surprised if either the DPJ or the LDP splinters over this issue. Perhaps both will.

If the revisionists can navigate these obstacles, one last challenge will remain: convincing the Japanese electorate that Article Nine should be changed. Public opinion is far more enthusiastic about constitutional revision in general than it is about changing Article Nine. In fact, in most polls, a majority of the public opposes revising Article Nine, although support for change has risen in recent years.[107] Moreover the public is deeply divided over collective self-defense.[108] The upshot is that although recent changes are trending the revisionists' way, public opinion remains opposed to revising Article Nine.

But the world is not standing still. With Japanese soldiers in harm's way half a world away, external events may overtake the slow-moving constitutional revision debate. If the SDF suffers casualties in Iraq, all sides will attempt to use them to support their position on Article Nine. How the public would respond is hard to predict. Similarly, one can imagine several regional crises that might have a major impact on Article Nine's future. The Korean peninsula and the Taiwan Straits come immediately to the fore. In the case of the former, a North Korean nuclear test would stimulate considerable support for the revisionist position, but it is not at all clear that a preemptive strike by the United States on the Yongbyon reactor would generate support for the alliance—or for changes to Article Nine. The Taiwan case is equally problematic. Now that Japan has publicly included the peaceful resolution of the Taiwan Straits issue among the list of "common strategic objectives" it shares with the U.S., a crisis there could push the Article Nine debate in different directions. A crisis precipitated by a Taiwanese declaration of independence would likely give the Japanese pause about the wisdom of government policy and could derail constitutional revision. One precipitated by another miscalculation by Beijing would likely be met with an accelerated revision of Article Nine.

With these remaining difficulties looming large, one might expect revisionists to give up on the grand project of constitutional revision and return to the tried-and-true method of reinterpretation. Several prominent politicians have in fact called for changing the interpretation to allow collective self-defense.[109] Immediately after taking office, Prime Minister Koizumi publicly considered formally enabling collective self-defense through reinterpretation but later abandoned the idea.[110] His decision was likely driven by several factors. First, revisionists believe they are closer to their goal than at any time in decades. Many politicians support revision because they think Japan should be able to exercise the same rights as other nations. If a reinterpretation were to resolve the long-standing dispute over collective self-defense, the entire revisionist movement would likely lose steam.[111]

> *Several prominent politicians have…called for changing the interpretation to allow collective self-defense*

Second, such a major change would not be on the same scale as past reinterpretations. Following the government interpretation in 1954, changes have come in the form of ever finer specifications of that interpretation's borders—defining such concepts as "offensive weapons" and "overseas deployment" as well as introducing such distinctions as "becoming one" with an attacker's force. Although the effect may have been to weaken the relevant constraint, none of these changes directly challenged the core of the 1954 interpretation—that Japan is limited in its use of force in ways that other countries are not. Issuing a reinterpretation allowing collective self-defense would in effect overthrow the 1954 interpretation, contradicting half a century of government policies. Revisionists would then not only have to justify this move to the public but would also have to reconcile it with the past actions of their own leadership. Koizumi, for example, has pointed to Article Nine as the reason Japan could not provide troops for major combat operations in Afghanistan and Iraq. How could he explain to Japanese allies and neighbors that these past decisions, along with five decades of LDP insistence that Japan could not engage in collective self-defense, were based on a mistaken interpretation of the constitution? Not only would this move look like a flagrant violation of the rule of law to domestic audiences, it would also complicate Japan's foreign relations.

Third, revisionists are well aware that reinterpretations, while easier to realize than amendments, are also more easily reversed. A future cabinet could simply return to the 1954 interpretation—or, worse, something more restrictive. With the DPJ vying for control of the Diet, the LDP is reluctant to give them such a controversial issue to use in the next election. In addition, such a radical reinterpretation would almost certainly prompt Kōmeitō to leave the ruling coalition, a blow that would cause the LDP serious legislative and electoral headaches. Fourth, and finally, there is little reason to expend political capital on reinterpretation when revision is in sight. Lacking both the legitimacy-building features (Diet votes, national referendum, and the like) and the institutional stickiness of formal amendment—and given a relatively elastic status quo—reinterpretation is thus not the favored solution for contemporary revisionists. If change is to come, it is likely to be in the form of constitutional revision.

As is the case with any political contest, the final outcome of the Article Nine debate will depend a great deal on the strategies chosen by participants. One important aspect of the strategies employed by those pushing to change Article Nine involves their treatment of other parts of the constitution. The fight over Article Nine is not taking place in a vacuum. It is only one issue, albeit a central one, in a wider debate over how the constitution should be changed. The major parties have all proposed revisions of various kinds. The LDP has so far been the most ambitious, calling for a complete rewriting (*zenmen kaitei*) that would reorder the entire document and include numerous changes and additions. This strategy, which was pursued by revisionists in the 1950s, apparently stems from two concerns. First, many conservatives still bristle that the current constitution is "U.S.-imposed" and blame it for what they see as the excessive individualism of contemporary Japanese society. For them, revision is an opportunity to redefine the nation and its values. Second, adopting an expansive approach allows revisionists to package less popular revisions, such as changes to Article Nine, with widely supported changes, such as the addition of new individual rights (Watanabe 2002: 45–50). In this view, putting more of the consti-

> *The fight over Article Nine is not taking place in a vacuum*

tution on the table may increase the ability of revisionists to link issues and horse-trade in the Diet while adding an attractive gloss to the revisionist project in the eyes of the public. A review of the LDP's November 2004 proposal shows this strategy at work. In addition to the significant changes to Article Nine discussed here, the proposal calls for major reforms in other categories. Importantly, the proposal calls for the establishment of new rights, including the right to personal privacy and the "right to know" (the right to access information from government organizations). These new rights are supported by both the DPJ and Kōmeitō and are also popular with the public.

These new individual rights may have been included as bargaining chips to allow the LDP to reach compromises on its less popular reforms. This would seem a sound strategy if Article Nine were the only controversial item on the LDP's constitutional agenda. It is not. The November proposal also addresses a wish list long held by LDP conservatives who think the current constitution has damaged Japan's traditional sense of national identity and social values. Reforms suggested in this area included reinstating the emperor as head of state (*genshu*), albeit one with no political power; incorporating language about patriotism (*aikokushin*) in the preamble; and adding duties (*gimu* or *sekimu*) to the citizenry, including the duty to defend the country. These reforms have been roundly criticized as "reactionary" by newspaper editorials and are not supported by the other major parties.[112] Not surprisingly, a recent *Asahi* poll found very little support for them among the public.[113]

Although the LDP revision proposal has yet to be finalized, internal preparations indicate movement toward a more accommodating stance. The LDP working draft circulated in November 2004 included several elements—such as provisions specifying Japan's nonnuclear policy and an explicit ban on conscription—that seem designed to appeal to the public and opposition parties. Although an outline prepared in April 2005 by a new committee established in mid-December by Prime Minister Koizumi and chaired by Mori Yoshirō unceremoniously dropped the nonnuclear language, it studiously avoided explicit recognition of the right of collective self-defense, opting instead to acknowledge the more general right of "*jiei*" (self-defense). This language remained intact when the Mori committee made public an updated version of the outline in early July.[114] The move appears designed to appeal to pragmatists within the party as well as to pacifists in Kōmeitō who are opposed to openly allowing collective self-defense. According to this strategy, once the "*jiei*" language has been added to the constitution, the issue of the recognition of the right of collective self-defense and the parameters of its exercise could be handled at a later date through interpretation and the passage of a basic defense law.[115] This outcome, however, would be ironic in the sense that revisionists who have long complained about using interpretation to affect constitutional change would in essence be creating the conditions for a future round of struggles over interpretation. In fact, any amendment that fails to specify the right of collective self-defense will almost certainly touch off a new era of constitutional governance through interpretation. Although such an outcome would likely end in some form of collective self-defense being recognized, continued conflict over this issue would be all but assured.

The July draft was more accommodating in other areas as well. For example, although the April draft specified a citizen's duty to defend the country (which might provide a legal justification for conscription), the July draft downgraded this controversial and politically unwise measure to a list of matters requiring "further discussion." In addition, the issue of whether to specify the Emperor as "head of state" (*genshu*), which resonates negatively among many Japanese as a reactionary nod to the prewar emperor system, was dropped completely from the July draft. Provided neither issue resurfaces in later LDP proposals, these changes are clear steps forward for the revision movement. One lesson from revisionists' failure in the 1950s was that the appearance of reactionary intentions has the potential to mobilize large cross-sections of the public against the entire revision project. A successful revision strategy would thus do well to steer clear of such measures.

Despite these compromises, however, the July outline is a deeply conservative document. The introduction of new rights, which were included in previous proposals, was set aside for further debate. In addition, the July outline retained language that in effect broadens the circumstances under which the government may abridge the basic rights of citizens. Currently the constitution limits basic freedoms such as those of speech and assembly only to the extent that they interfere with the "public welfare" (*kōkyō no fukushi*). While the November draft expanded this exception by replacing "public welfare" with the vague "public values" (*kōkyō no kachi*), the April draft went even further—suggesting that basic rights may be abridged for a variety of reasons including the pursuit of the "public interest" (*kōeki*) or the strengthening of "public order" (*ōyake no chitsujo*). This provision remained unchanged in the July draft. The drive to limit basic freedoms may prove problematic for the revision movement if it appears in the final LDP proposal. Although establishing a strong initial negotiating position is an important concern for the LDP, limiting basic freedoms is a nonstarter that will allow opponents to demonize the process as antidemocratic. Its retention in the November LDP proposal would reduce the chances of successful revision.

A second important strategic issue for revisionists involves the crafting of the revision procedure bills. Negotiations are ongoing to invest the Diet constitutional research commissions with the power to consider this legislation. In addition to measures to cover debate in the Diet, a law establishing the national referendum must also be passed. Although there are many issues at stake in setting up these procedures, revisionists may pursue two basic strategies. They may try to establish a system in which amendments to multiple articles may be considered simultaneously and voted up or down with a single vote or one in which multiple amendments are considered, and voted on, one at a time. The former approach would coincide with the *zenmen kaitei* strategy described earlier, and there are signs the LDP may prefer this position. When a coalition government committee chaired by the head of the LDP constitution research committee drafted a proposal for a national referendum law in December 2004, it left open the possibility that multiple amendments might be bundled together in a single vote.[116] This strategy contrasts with an April 2005 proposal put forth by the DPJ that explicitly called for citizens to be given the opportunity to vote separately on different proposed amendments.[117]

In our view, adopting a procedure in which changes to multiple articles are determined in a single vote will ultimately be counterproductive for the revisionists. First, the risk-averse Japanese electorate will likely balk if given a single vote on changes as diverse as the language of the preamble, duties and rights of the citizen, the role of the emperor, and Article Nine. Second, this procedure would create a powerful temptation for conservatives to pursue long-held (but wildly unpopular) goals such as limiting basic freedoms. This strategy is thus likely to generate opponents both in the Diet and among the public. Allowing parliamentarians and the public to assess changes on an article-by-article (or least topic-by-topic) basis is both more likely to succeed and better for Japanese democracy. It would engender less widespread opposition, reduce the public's suspicion of the process, and allow for a clearer and more accessible public debate. The demands of this procedure would also likely moderate revision proposals—eliminating radical positions with little chance of passage at an early stage. In sum, then, the initial strategic decisions made by revisionists will be vital to the eventual success of the process and may be viewed as indicators of the likelihood of change.

So what is going to happen? Reliable methods of predicting major institutional change have so far eluded social science. With all the appropriate caveats, the Article Nine debate has four possible outcomes. First, it seems likely that any change will at least formalize the informal status quo. All major parties and *the Article Nine debate has four possible outcomes* the public agree that Japan has the right to defend itself and may maintain the SDF for this purpose. Kōmeitō has argued that making these points explicit is unnecessary, but both the LDP and the DPJ support adding language clarifying the SDF's role and the nation's right to self-defense. Although this change would simply elevate the 1954 interpretation to constitutional status, it might be used to break the taboo associated with revision and Article Nine, paving the way for more extensive changes in the future. And this revision may have a particular appeal in Japanese politics, since it is in effect a face-saving way to paint the status quo with the brush of reform.

A second likelihood is that the major parties will reach an agreement on allowing a restricted form of collective self-defense. An Article Nine revised in this way would recognize the right of individual self-defense and some limited form of collective self-defense linked to the U.S.-Japan alliance, to the United Nations, or both. The key event in this scenario would be a compromise between the LDP and the DPJ over how to restrict collective self-defense. If such an agreement could be reached, and the conditions were sufficiently restrictive, it seems possible that even Kōmeitō might sign on. A grand compromise of this proportion would also ease the measure's passage in the national referendum.

The third and least likely possibility is the formal recognition of the right of collective self-defense without any specific limitations. Although the LDP proposal for Article Nine is currently in this form, it will be interesting to see if it survives intact in the party's final draft. Considering the amount of debate within the party, the level of incongruence with the positions of Kōmeitō and DPJ, and the public's misgivings on this issue, this proposal seems unlikely to overcome the opposition it faces. Its best chance of passage would involve making major concessions by adding restrictions to a relevant subconstitutional law, such as a new basic defense law. Although this law would be easier to change, the operational result, at least for the time being, would be the same.

It should also be noted that the possibility of complete failure continues to loom over the entire project. The institutional requirements are high and the Diet and the public are anything but united on the key issues. The current revision movement may well fail in the Diet—either because of the failure to reach a consensus on draft language or a disagreement about which revision strategy to employ. Nevertheless we observe an encouraging irony for democracy in Japan. In the past, the key obstacles to revising Article Nine were pragmatists in the LDP, pacifists in the opposition, and a divided public. If pragmatism and pacifism continue to decline in the Diet, the role of the public will become greater than ever. If the public continues to oppose major changes in Article Nine, the electorate may remain an important force in the constitutional debate. Thus while the final outcome remains uncertain, two aspects of the process are very certain indeed. First, Article Nine's future will be as contested as its past. And second, the constitutional debate is shaping up to become a major test for Japanese democracy—one that the Japanese people have given every indication of passing with flying colors.

And, finally, there is always the possibility of new group formation. One such possibility is the development of a Gaullist movement seeking to revise Article Nine in concert with an expansion of Japanese defensive capabilities outside the confines of the U.S.-Japan alliance. Although some polls show a cooling of public opinion toward the alliance and many senior politicians see strengthening ties with regional partners as a means of enhancing Japan's position vis-à-vis the United States, there is little evidence to suggest broad-based support for a radical break in security policy at this time (Heginbotham and Samuels 2002a: 119). This is not to say that anti-American sentiments are unheard of in the halls of the Diet or that there are no areas of divergence in U.S. and Japanese foreign policy preferences. There were strong anti-American undercurrents in the DPJ critique of Koizumi's response to the Iraq War, and LDP backbenchers sometimes share these sentiments. Likewise preferences on how to deal with Tehran—like preferences on how to deal with Pyongyang—have been subject to intense debate between Tokyo and Washington. Neither these views nor these divergences have challenged the mainstream of the revisionist movement, however, which continues to operate under the assumption of a robust alliance.

Implications

If Article Nine is revised to allow for collective self-defense, it will certainly have major implications for Japan, the United States, and the East Asian region. Domestically the road to collective self-defense may touch off another round of political realignment with both the LDP and the DPJ splitting and reforming along pro-revision and anti-revision lines. Or it may result in a grand compromise that unifies all major parties and heralds a new era of Japanese politics in which the central cleavage shifts from foreign to domestic policy. Either way, it is hard to imagine how such an accomplishment would not shake up the Japanese political world for years to come.

The impact on U.S.-Japan relations will depend a great deal on the details of the revision. The United States has abandoned its Cold War "dual containment" approach to its alliance with Japan. Since the first Gulf War, the United States has increased pressure on Japan to make more substantive contributions to the alliance. Deputy Secretary of State Richard Armitage reportedly suggested in mid-2004 that Article Nine was an obstacle to Japanese membership on the UN Security Council.[118] It seems clear the United States would like to see Japan free from the present restraints of Article Nine. Yet the old adage about being careful what one wishes for could easily apply here. For example, if Article Nine is revised but

the United States would like to see Japan free [of] the...restraints of Article Nine

new restrictions continue to keep Japan from providing troops for future U.S.-led "coalitions of the willing," relations may suffer more than if no constitutional change occurred at all. At present, Japanese administrations may make the plausible claim that Article Nine ties their hands. This claim loses much of its force, however, once Article Nine has been revised in a way that still fails to allow Japan to fight shoulder to shoulder with its key ally.

Still worse, the United States may have to face the eventuality of a Japan constitutionally capable of providing combat forces but politically unwilling to do so. The example of Germany is instructive in this regard.

In 1991, West Germany pointed to constitutional constraints to avoid participating in combat operations in Iraq (although it offered other forms of support). During the mid-1990s, the German Constitutional Court ruled that military operations outside the North American Treaty Organization (NATO) area were constitutional (Itoh 1998: 167–68). Germany then provided combat forces for the war in Kosovo and, more recently, has played a large role in the occupation of Afghanistan. The German refusal to contribute forces for the U.S.-led invasion of Iraq in 2003, however, placed intense strain on the alliance that is still playing out. Politicians in the United States have demonized German leaders; alliance relations deteriorated to the lowest level in twenty years (and perhaps ever); and plans for shifting U.S. bases out of Germany are in the offing. By comparison, Japan participated in none of the above conflicts and has paid little price in the context of the U.S.-Japan alliance. Although Japan's noncombat participation in the postwar occupation of Iraq has provided "boots on the ground," the fact remains that Japan refused to bleed with the United States against Iraq's armies. Even so, commentators agree that U.S.-Japan relations have never been better, while the news of President Bush's recent trip to Europe was all about "reconciliation" and trying to "repair the damage" to the transatlantic alliance.

In short, saying no because one can't and saying no because one won't are not the same thing and can have different consequences for alliance relations. In Japan's case, there is a particularly large difference between a refusal based on a U.S.-imposed constitutional provision dripped in tragic history and a refusal resulting from an active choice. Thus, almost paradoxically, U.S.-Japan relations may well worsen if major changes are made to Article Nine. In any event, Japan will remain the junior partner in the alliance and will need to find new ways to hedge the dual risks of entrapment and abandonment.

Japan's regional relations are likely to suffer in the wake of any Article Nine revision. South Koreans are none too happy with the proposed change but—sandwiched as they are between China and the U.S.-Japan alliance—are likely to resign themselves to it. Still, media commentaries on the LDP November draft were provocative. Yonhap Television News said that if the Japanese constitution is revised, "Japan will be armed with military power and begin marching toward becoming a great military power."[119] *Munhwa Ilbo* called the LDP draft "shocking" and worried that by revising the constitution Japan would join the ranks of great military powers such as the United States, China, and Russia. And one commentator from the moderate *Chungang Ilbo* was even more blunt: "For the past 60 years, Japan wasn't really its true self. It was constrained by the bridle of defeat under the peace constitution. However, we will see the real Japan soon."[120] There is thus the possibility that South Korea would use a major revision of Article Nine to justify a more friendly posture toward China or perhaps, at the least, a more independent stance toward the United States and Japan. In either case, Japan would clearly have some diplomacy ahead of it.

China's reaction certainly was predictable. Many in Beijing will find this change very provocative—and not for no reason. Xinhua News Agency declared that the LDP draft

> is a signal that warrants the vigilance of the world, especially various Asian countries that were invaded by Japan in the past. . . . Japan is daydreaming to materialize its wild ambitions of becoming a political and military power. Japan will then definitely pose a serious threat to peace in Asia and the world. In the future, it is absolutely possible for a country that has been unable and unwilling to admit its past history of invading other countries to repeat its historic mistakes. Once Japan has broken through the restrictions stipulated in the peaceful constitution, Japan's "self-defense military force" will freely go to various places around the world and wantonly launch "preemptive" strikes on its so-called enemies. Such a scenario can only make the peoples of various Asian countries that previously suffered the cruel oppression of Japanese militarists maintain their heightened vigilance.[121]

The questions are how Beijing—now Japan's largest trading partner—will use a Japanese constitutional change, for how long, and at what cost? Surely it will be a tool for anti-Japanese public diplomacy. Likewise, it is a good bet that Beijing will continue to use it to denounce Tokyo to help consolidate power at home. But when does this strategy become counterproductive? Do the anti-Japanese demonstrations of April 2005 prefigure domestic instability Beijing will be unable to control? And so long as it is "hugging the U.S. close" (Riddell 2003), why should Japan care? Still, Article Nine revision, even of the cosmetic variety, will complicate Japan's relations with its neighbors.

In sum, then, the constitutional stalemate over Article Nine is into its sixth decade. In recent years, however, the battle lines of the debate have shifted in ways that make major change imaginable. Although this shift has neither set the future course of change nor guaranteed its occurrence, it has increased the likelihood that the dispute over Article Nine will break out of its long-standing political bottleneck and finally allow the Japanese people a say in its resolution. Whatever the outcome, we believe the upcoming struggle will be an important, and hopefully affirmative, experience for Japan's democracy.

the battle lines of the debate have shifted in ways that make major change imaginable

Endnotes

Parts of this essay previously appeared in the following publications: Richard J. Samuels, "Politics, Security Policy, and Japan's Cabinet Legislation Bureau: Who Elected These Guys, Anyway?", Japan Policy Research Institute Working Paper 99 (March 2004); Richard J. Samuels and J. Patrick Boyd, "Kenpō Kyūjō ni mo Kyūshō Ari?—Kenpō Ronsō no Yukue" (Does Article Nine Have Nine Lives?: The Future of the Constitutional Debate in Japan), *Ronza* (April, 2004); and J. Patrick Boyd, "Nine Lives: Pragmatism, Pacifism, and Japan's Article Nine" (master's thesis, MIT, 2003). In addition, the authors are grateful for the feedback received after Samuels presented these ideas at the Brookings Institution Center for Northeast Asia Policy Studies (December 2004), Harvard University's Program on U.S.-Japan Relations (April 2005), and the Center for Strategic and International Studies (June 2005). All Japanese names appear in Japanese order, with surname first.

1. Interview with Watanabe Osamu, Tokyo, May 31, 2005.

2. Movement "strength" is measured here on three dimensions: (1) the presence or absence of a formal government process (such as interparty committees and commissions) dedicated to discussing constitutional issues; (2) proliferation of large numbers of revision proposals in the public domain; and (3) polling data suggesting a large portion of the public amenable to revision. The two cases meet these conditions as follows: (1) the Commission on the Constitution was established in 1956 and operated under the cabinet office between 1957 and 1964, while special committees mandated to discuss constitutional issues were established in both houses of the Diet in 1999, beginning operation in 2000 with a five-year tenure; (2) according to one historian's count, nineteen major proposals for constitutional revision were produced during each of the periods 1947–64 and 1990–2002, while only four such proposals emerged during the intervening years (Watanabe 2002: 19); and (3) these two periods were the only times when public support for constitutional revision approached or exceeded 50 percent. See Fukui (1970: 214); *Yomiuri Shimbun*, April 2, 2003.

3. Schlichtmann (1995: 33–67). Note that Article Nine is modeled on the Kellog-Briand Pact of 1928 and that both Italy and Germany voluntarily adopted war renunciation clauses in their postwar constitutions.

4. In addition to MacArthur, the GS officers most involved in editing and interpreting what became Article Nine were Brigadier General Courtney Whitney and Colonel Charles Kades.

5. For firsthand accounts of GHQ's understanding of Article Nine see MacArthur (1964: 304) and Kades (1989: 236–37).

6. Maki (1964: 305, 298–365). Examples include the Suzuki case (1952), in which the Supreme Court refused to consider a legislator's claim that the National Police Reserves violated Article Nine on the grounds that the court could not interpret law outside the bounds of a concrete case, and the Sunakawa case (1959), in which the court argued it could not determine the constitutionality of the U.S.-Japan Security Treaty due to its "highly political nature" (*kōdo no seijisei wo yū suru mono*).

7. Nakamura (2001: 9–10, 106). Although the "modern warfare" standard was proposed by CLB Director-General Satō Tatsuo, some senior CLB members, including Hayashi Shūzō, who would become the next director-general, and Takatsuji Masaki, who served as deputy director-general, disagreed with the rationale behind it. They would move to make changes as soon as Satō stepped down.

8. For more on Yoshida's remarkably creative leadership see Samuels (2003a: chap. 8).

9. Nakamura (2001: 142–46). Note that this decision also became the baseline for February 2003 reminders by JDA Director-General Ishiba Shigeru that Japan retains the right to use force to preempt a North Korean attack.

10. *Voice*, December 2001.

11. Ibid.

12. When discussing security issues, Japanese officials have taken pains to distinguish between "collective self-defense" (*shūdanteki jiei*) and "collective security" (*shūdanteki anzenhoshō*). The distinction rests on two points: whether the use of force is involved and whether the mission involves the security of an ally (and thus, indirectly, Japan's own self-defense) or the security of countries without alliances with Japan. Collective self-defense is narrowly defined as the *use of force* to defend an *ally* that has come under attack. The focus here is on bilateral military cooperation, which is banned under the extant interpretation of Article Nine. Collective security, by contrast, refers to cooperation with international organizations and other countries to enhance the security of countries without relevant alliance relationships. Collective security may or may not involve the use of force. Taken from the United Nations Charter, this concept refers to multilateral cooperation that may include diplomatic, economic, and military action. The government interpretation of Article Nine allows Japan to engage in the diplomatic and economic aspects of collective security but forbids the use of force even in this multilateral situation. Thus, at present, Japan could not participate in a UN army (if one were formed) that required the use of force to accomplish its mission. For references to this distinction see *Yomiuri Shimbun*, May 3, 1997; Nakamura (2001: 255–57; and Asagumo Shimbunsha (2003: 557–62, 571).

13. *Sankei Shimbun*, December 29, 2001.

14. Quoted in National Institute for Defense Studies (2002: 315).

15. *Japan Economic Newswire*, March 15, 2005.

16. For an analysis of the Japanese military's compliance with Article Nine interpretations see Boyd (2003). For assessments of the roles and capabilities of the Japanese military in the 1970s and post-Cold War period, see Auer (1973), Twomey (2000), and Lind (2004).

17. For versions of this argument see Layne (1993), Menon (1997), Hughes (2004), and Waltz (1993; 2000).

18. See *National Defense Program Guideline, FY 2005-*, December 10, 2004 (www.kantei.go.jp/foreign/policy/2004/1210taikou_e.html). Please note that the earlier editions of this plan were referred to as the National Defense Program Outline (NDPO). Although the document's Japanese name remains the same, the Government of Japan changed the last word of the English name to "guideline" beginning with the 2004 plan. We adopt this nomenclature here but continue to refer to earlier plans by their original names.

19. For more on the "alliance security dilemma" see Snyder (1984). For an application to Japan see Unger (1997).

20. For this argument see Christensen (1999) and Friedberg (1993–94).

21. On this last point see *Joint Statement of the US-Japan Security Consultative Committee*, February 19, 2005 (http://japan.usembassy.gov/e/p/tp-20050219-77.html).

22. *Asahi Shimbun*, April 22 and May 6, 2002.

23. See, for example, Kunihiro (1997) and Green (2001: 25, 46).

24. These figures are calculated from the authors' analysis of data from the *Yomiuri* 2002 Diet poll; see *Yomiuri Shimbun*, March 22, 2002.

25. *Asahi Shimbun*, May 1, 2004.

26. *NHK*, May 2002.

27. This is not to say that generational differences have never been a factor in the constitutional revision debate. Important differences may indeed have existed in past years. The point here is simply that generational differences are not as significant in the contemporary Article Nine debate as is often asserted. Thus generational change (in the form of cohort replacement) is unlikely to be the major driver behind the rise of revisionism during this period.

28. For example, historian Kōsaka Masataka (1968: 64–71) is critical of Yoshida for failing to redefine national identity in line with his security policy.

29. Although commonly associated with the wartime militarist regime through government documents such as *Kokutai no Hongi* (1937), the basic elements of this identity were codified in early Meiji-era works such as the Imperial Rescript on Education (1890). It is thus important to note that this national conception was a prominent part of identity politics long before it was seized upon by the militarists of the 1930s.

30. For more on the pragmatists see Dower (1979: 318–20) and Ōtake (1988: 59–69).

31. Samuels (1994) and Pyle (1997). The view that security derives from prosperity contrasts strongly with common American appraisals of this relationship, which position security as a prerequisite for prosperity. In a recent example, the Bush administration, in announcing the Security and Prosperity Partnership of North America, declared that this trilateral agreement between Canada, the United States, and Mexico was based on the "principle that our prosperity is dependent on our security." See White House Fact Sheet, March 23, 2005 (www.whitehouse.gov/news/releases/2005/03/20050323-4.html).

32. Once the country had been returned to prosperity, Yoshida and his group thought further investment in military preparedness could be considered. See Pyle (1996: 23–28).

33. For discussions of the pragmatist position see Pyle (1996: 26) and Kōsaka (1968: 66).

34. For more on this group's thought see the writings of Maruyama Masao, particularly Maruyama (1963: 290–320). For an overview see Hook (1996: 26–41).

35. Yoshida's negotiating strategy is discussed in Dower (1979: 377–400) and Kataoka (1991: 82).

36. Kataoka (1991: 91). For an account of this episode see Igarashi (1985: 350).

37. Cole et al. (1958: 466). For accounts of the constitutional debate during the mid-1950s see Fukui (1970: 212–14), Maki (1962: 132), and Watanabe (2002: 421–40).

38. Kataoka (1991: 169–74) and Packard (1966: 47). There were several criticisms of the security pact: it did not include a specific U.S. guarantee of Japan's external security; it allowed U.S. troops to quell internal disturbances; and the United States could adjust its forces in Japan without prior consultation with Japanese authorities.

39. Hara (1988: 176–77) and Kataoka (1991: 190). See Samuels (2003a: chap. 9) for an analysis of Kishi's transwar political career.

40. Hara (1988: 245). For a recent reprint of the interview in question see Watanabe (2002: 590–93).

41. For relevant accounts see Hara (1988: 346–50), Kataoka (1991: 193, 198–200), and Nakamura (2001: 181–85).

42. This group included LDP Secretary-General Ozawa Ichirō, LDP General Council Nishioka Takeo, LDP Policy Affairs Research Council leader Katō Mutsuki, and Watanabe Michio, the leader of a major LDP faction, among others. See Unger (1997: 152) and Purrington and A. K. (1991: 316).

43. Revisionist politicians who have called for allowing collective self-defense include former Prime Minister Nakasone Yasuhiro, the faction of former Prime Minister Hashimoto Ryūtarō, Yamazaki Taku, and Prime Minister Koizumi Junichirō—all of the LDP—as well as Hatoyama Yukio and Ozawa Ichirō of the DPJ.

44. Approximately 40 percent of LDP Diet members are second- or third-generation politicians, while many prominent opposition leaders are as well. Examples include Abe Shinzō, Fukuda Yasuo, Ozawa Ichirō, Kōno Yōhei, and Hatoyama Yukio. See *Mainichi Shimbun,* May 1, 2003.

45. See, for example, the pro-revision positions of the LDP party platform and LDP Commission on the Constitution.

46. Katō (1998: 163). Examples include the Jishu Kenpō Seitei Kokumin Kaigi, founded by Kishi Nobusuke in 1969; the Jishu Kenpō Kisei Giin Dōmei, led until recently by Kimura Mitsuo; and the Institute for International Policy Studies, established by Nakasone Yasuhiro in 1988.

47. Examples include the LDP Commission on the Constitution's revision reports issued in 1972 and 1982 and the Jishu Kenpō Kisei Giin Dōmei's constitutional revision proposals published in 1981 and 1982.

48. Kunihiro (1997). Murayama's decision followed a decade of erosion in the consensus surrounding the JSP's security stances. For a brief summary of this period see Hook and McCormack (2001: 29).

49. Current SDPJ rhetoric is replete with "peace nation" references. In addition to traditional exhortations to "pacifist Japan" (*heiwa kokka toshite no Nihon*), they also call for making Japan a "model peace nation" (*heiwa moderu koku*) and exporting the peace constitution to the world. For examples see the SDPJ website: www.www5.sdp.or.jp/central/062topics.html (May 2, 2003).

50. Party Platform, Third Kōmeitō National Conference at www.komei.or.jp/policy/detail/001.htm (May 2, 2003).

51. Curtis (1999: 188–203). See also the interview with Murayama Tomiichi in *Asahi Shimbun*, January 23, 2002.

52. For examples see the statements by Yokomichi Takahiro and Hironaka Wakako at www.yokomichi.com/monthly_message/2000.11.01.htm (November 1, 2000) and www.dpj.or.jp/news/200303/20030320_08hironaka.html (March 20, 2003).

53. This estimate considers the post-2003 election strengths of these parties and factions.

54. For more on these policies see Boyd (2003: 37–50) and Chai (1997: 389–412).

55. For more on the institutional role of the CLB in interpreting Article Nine see Samuels (2004), Nakamura (2001), and Nishikawa (2000).

56. One such example is the Research Institute for Peace and Security, founded by Professor Inoki Masamichi, the principal author of the *1980 Report on Comprehensive National Security*.

57. A *Yomiuri Shimbun* editorial praising the passage of the bill nonetheless emphasized the need to go further by reinterpreting the constitution to allow for collective self-defense. See *Yomiuri Shimbun*, May 25, 1999.

58. *Nihon Keizai Shimbun*, May 16, 1999; *NHK*, May 24, 1999, FBIS, Document ID: FTS19990524000618; *Mainichi Shimbun*, May 25, 1999; *Shūkan Asahi*, June 18, 1999, FBIS, Document ID: FTS19990617001886.

59. For an example of an Article Nine revision proposal by a young scholar see Kitaoka (1999: 126–35).

60. *Daily Yomiuri*, March 22, 2002.

61. For more on the contrast between the Italian and Japanese communist parties see Samuels (2003a: 299–315).

62. For an account of Nakasone's campaign against public-sector unions see Samuels (2003b).

63. For more on the JCP's travails see Samuels (2003a: 310–13).

64. Factions continue to play an important role in the allocation of party and government posts below the cabinet minister level, and there is evidence that Koizumi recently turned to factional leaders to replace a resigning cabinet member. See Krauss and Pekkanen (2004: 13–17).

65. *Nihon Keizai Shimbun*, November 13, 2003.

66. *Yomiuri Shimbun*, July 14, 2004.

67. *Asahi Shimbun*, October 6, 2001.

68. *Daily Yomiuri*, March 22, 2002.

69. It should be noted that the SDF dispatch was only part of Japan's overall response. It is highlighted here, however, because of its particular relevance to Article Nine. For a comprehensive treatment see Heginbotham and Samuels (2002b).

70. This group combined members from the Cabinet Secretariat, MOFA, JDA, and National Police Agency (NPA).

71. Note that this decision was reversed and the Aegis-equipped ships were dispatched in December 2002. See *Mainichi Shimbun*, December 15, 2002.

72. For an English translation of the Ozawa Committee's report see LDP (1992).

73. Koizumi's approval rating was an atmospheric 79 percent during the debate over the Antiterrorism Law. In addition, 70 percent of the public was in favor of Japan supporting U.S. military action. As the issue turned to Iraq, however, the public's views shifted dramatically. On the eve of the war, Koizumi's approval rating was down to the low 40s, with an even smaller percentage of the public supporting his initial position on Iraq. During the debate over the Iraq Reconstruction bill in the Diet, the public's support for the Iraq deployment actually fell from 46 percent in June to 33 percent in July. Opposition rose over this period from 43 percent to 55 percent. See *Nihon Keizai Shimbun*, September 25, 2001; *Mainichi Shimbun*, March 21, 2003; *Asahi Shimbun*, March 22, 2003; *Nihon Keizai Shimbun*, March 21, 2003; and *Asahi Shimbun*, July 21, 2003.

74. In addition to Ōmori, the group included ten staff members mainly from the JDA and MOFA. See Shinoda (2004: 102–3).

75. These two committees were the Yotō Iraku Kitachōsen Mondai Renraku Kyōgikai and the Kinkyū Tero Taisaku Honbu.

76. This account is drawn largely from Shinoda (2004: 105–9).

77. *Asahi Shimbun*, July 4 and July 25, 2003.

78. JPP20041213000020, *Tokyo Kyodo World Service in English*, December 13, 2004.

79. *Asahi Shimbun*, November 3, 2003; *Yomiuri Shimbun*, June 20, 2004.

80. *Yomiuri Shimbun*, June 20, 2004.

81. *Asahi Shimbun*, April 4, 2005; *Asahi Shimbun*, July 7, 2005.

82. *Yomiuri Shimbun*, March 17, 2004.

83. *Asahi Shimbun*, November 3, 2003; *Yomiuri Shimbun*, June 20, 2004.

84. This was another "gift" to the revisionists from Yoshida. Although the Home Affairs Agency submitted a revision procedure bill to the cabinet in 1953, Yoshida's cabinet refused to approve it. See *Daily Yomiuri*, January 8, 2002.

85. *Sankei Shimbun*, March 12, 2005.

86. *Yomiuri Shimbun*, October 13, 2002; *Daily Yomiuri*, March 22, 2002.

87. *Yomiuri Shimbun*, March 17, 2004.

88. *Nihon Keizai Shimbun*, February 17, 2005.

89. *Nihon Keizai Shimbun*, March 15, 2005.

90. *Yomiuri Shimbun*, April 2, 2004; *Asahi Shimbun*, May 1, 2004.

91. The lower house panel comprised 26 parliamentarians from the LDP, 18 from the DPJ, 4 from Kōmeitō, and 1 each from the JCP and SDP. According to newspaper accounts, a "majority opinion" required that at least two-thirds of the panel must support a position. It should be noted that the JCP and SDP, whose panel members did not sign off on the report, argued that the panel leadership constructed opinions in such an abstract way as to guarantee large levels of support for revision but mask important differences of opinion. See *Yomiuri Shimbun*, March 23, 2005; *Japan Times*, April 16, 2005.

92. *Asahi Shimbun*, March 26, 2005.

93. *Asahi Shimbun*, April 20, 2005.

94. *Daily Yomiuri*, April 22, 2005; *Sankei Shimbun*, April 21, 2005.

95. Kōmeitō, *Daigokaitōzenkoku Taikai Undō Hōshin* (Fifth Party National Convention Action Plan), October 31, 2004.

96. *Yomiuri Shimbun*, June 20, 2004.

97. *Asahi Shimbun*, June 19, 2004.

98. *Mainichi Shimbun*, November 11, 2003.

99. For a recent reference to this intraparty dispute see *Nihon Keizai Shimbun*, January 8, 2005.

100. Quoted in *Chūō Kōron*, June 2002, pp. 65–69, FBIS, Document ID: JPP20020517000008 (emphasis added); see also Yamasaki (2001: 77–78).

101. This scheme was floated by Kamei Shizuka in February 2001; see *Asagumo*, February 15, 2001, FBIS, Document ID: JPP20010223000063. Kamei explained: "If our ally, the United States, should come under attack, our nation's right of collective self-defense could be exercised based on the US-Japan Security Treaty. . . . However, when the United States gets involved in the regional disputes of other countries because of an emergency in the area surrounding Japan, we cannot lend a hand by dispatching SDF units overseas as a military force. . . . Since the SDF could not be dispatched in case of an intervention in a regional dispute, we cannot exercise the right as a general rule."

102. *Mainichi Shimbun*, March 15, 2005. There is also a disagreement within the LDP over the degree to which these rights should be made explicit in the constitution. Some fear that specifying individual and collective self-defense rights will lead to demands that other matters be spelled out in excessive detail in the constitution; others worry that failing to do so might allow later administrations to change them through reinterpretation. See *Nihon Keizai Shimbun*, January 8, 2005.

103. *Asahi Shimbun*, January 31, 2005 and June 28, 2005.

104. In April 2005, Edano Yukio, chairman of the DPJ constitutional research committee, released a new summary of the committee's internal discussions. Although Edano claimed there was no change in the party's position on collective security, the summary removed the explicit reference to allowing the use of force in UN-sanctioned operations that appeared in the June 2004 report. Pro-revision editorialists characterized this as a step back for the party's constitutional position and expressed concern that the DPJ might be positioning itself to use differences in constitutional positions to attack the LDP during the next lower house election. See *Yomiuri Shimbun*, April 29, 2005.

105. *Asahi Shimbun*, December 14, 2001.

106. *Yomiuri Shimbun*, June 20, 2004.

107. *Asahi Shimbun*, May 1, 2004; *NHK*, May 2002.

108. *Asahi Shimbun*, May 1, 2004; *Yomiuri Shimbun*, April 1, 2003.

109. Abe Shinzō, former LDP secretary-general, is one such politician.

110. *Asahi Shimbun*, October 6, 2001.

111. Interview with former Japan Defense Agency Director-General Aiichi Kazuo, April 17, 2002.

112. *Mainichi Shimbun*, November 21, 2004.

113. *Asahi Shimbun*, May 1, 2004.

114. *Asahi Shimbun*, July 7, 2005; The full document is available at: www.jimin.jp/jimin/shin_kenpou/index.html.

115. *Asahi Shimbun*, April 4, 2005; interview with Watanabe Osamu, Tokyo, May 31, 2005.

116. *Yomiuri Shimbun*, December 1, 2004. For a critique of the December proposal see Nihon Bengoshi Rengōkai (2005: 2–3).

117. *Yomiuri Shimbun*, April 25, 2005.

118. *Asahi Shimbun*, July 23, 2004.

119. JPP20041117000077, *Tokyo Kyodo World Service in English*, November 17, 2004.

120. KPP20041122000136, *Chungang Ilbo in English*, November 23, 2004.

121. CPP20041119000103, *Xinhua Domestic Service in Chinese*, November 19, 2004.

Bibliography

Asagumo Shimbunsha. 2003. *Bōei Handobukku* (Defense Handbook). Tokyo: Asagumo Shimbunsha.

Auer, James E. 1973. *The Postwar Rearmament of Japanese Maritime Forces, 1945–71.* New York: Praeger.

Benfell, Steven. 1998. "Meet the New Japan, Same as the Old Japan: The History and Politics of Postwar National Identity." Paper for the Program for U.S.-Japan Relations. Cambridge, MA: Center for International Affairs and Reischauer Institute of Japanese Studies.

Berger, Tom. 1993. "From Sword to Chrysanthemum: Japan's Culture of Anti-militarism." *International Security* 47(4): 119–50.

———. 1996. "Norms, Identity, and National Security in Germany and Japan." In Peter Katzenstein, ed., *The Culture of National Security: Norms and Identity in World Politics.* New York: Columbia University Press.

———. 1998. *Cultures of Antimilitarism.* Baltimore: Johns Hopkins University Press.

Boyd, J. Patrick. 2003. "Nine Lives: Pragmatism, Pacifism, and Japan's Article Nine." Master's thesis. Cambridge, MA: MIT, Department of Political Science.

Chai, Sun-Ki. 1997. "Entrenching the Yoshida Doctrine: Three Techniques for Institutionalization." *International Organization* 51(3): 389–412.

Christensen, Thomas. 1999. "China, the U.S.-Japan Alliance, and the Security Dilemma in East Asia." *International Security* 23(4): 49–80.

Cole, Allan, et al. 1958. *Japanese Opinion Polls with Socio-Political Significance 1947–1957.* Medford, MA: Tufts University/Williams College.

Cox, Gary, Francis Rosenbluth, and Michael Thies. 1999. "Electoral Reform and the Fate of Factions: The Case of Japan's Liberal Democratic Party." *British Journal of Political Science* 29(1): 33–56.

Curtis, Gerald. 1999. *The Logic of Japanese Politics*. New York: Columbia University Press.

Dower, John. 1979. *Empire and Aftermath*. Cambridge, MA: Council of East Asian Studies, Harvard University.

Friedberg, Aaron. 1993–94. "Ripe for Rivalry: Prospects for Peace in Multipolar Asia." *International Security* 8(3): 5–33.

Fukui, Haruhiro. 1970. *Party in Power: The Japanese Liberal Democrats and Policy-Making*. Berkeley: University of California Press.

Glosserman, Brad. 2005. "Planning Ahead." *Comparative Connections* 6(4): 23–28.

Green, Michael. 2001. *Japan's Reluctant Realism*. New York: Palgrave.

Hara, Yoshihisa. 1988. *Sengo Nihon to Kokusai Seiji: Ampō Kaitei no Seijirikigaku* (Postwar Japan and International Politics: The Political Dynamics of the Security Treaty Revision). Tokyo: Chūō Kōronsha.

Heginbotham, Eric, and Richard J. Samuels. 2002a. "Japan's Dual Hedge." *Foreign Affairs* 81(5): 110–21.

———. 2002b. "Japan." In Richard Ellings and Aaron Friedberg, eds., *Strategic Asia 2002–03*. Seattle: National Bureau of Asian Research.

Hirano, Sadao. 1996. *Ozawa Ichiro to no Nijū Nen* (Twenty Years with Ichiro Ozawa). Tokyo: Purejidentosha.

Hook, Glenn. 1996. *Militarization and Demilitarization in Contemporary Japan*. London: Routledge.

Hook, Glenn, and Gavan McCormack. 2001. *Japan's Contested Constitution: Documents and Analysis*. London: Routledge.

Hughes, Christopher W. 2002. "Japan's Security Policy and the War on Terror: Steady Incrementalism or Radical Leap?" CSGR Working Paper 104/02. Warwick: University of Warwick, CSGR.

———. 2004. *Japan's Reemergence as a Normal Military Power*. Adelphi Paper 368–69. London: Institute for International Strategic Studies.

Igarashi, Takeshi. 1985. "Peace-Making and Party Politics: The Formation of the Domestic Foreign-Policy System in Postwar Japan." *Journal of Japanese Studies* 11(2): 323–56.

Itoh, Mayumi. 1998. *Globalization of Japan: Japanese Sakoku Mentality and U.S. Efforts to Open Japan*. New York: St. Martin's Press.

Kades, Charles. 1989. "The American Role in Revising Japan's Imperial Constitution." *Political Science Quarterly* 104(2): 215–47.

Kahn, Herman. 1970. *The Emerging Japanese Superstate: Challenge and Response*. Englewood Cliffs, N.J.: Prentice-Hall, Inc.

Kataoka, Tetsuya. 1991. *The Price of a Constitution: The Origin of Japan's Postwar Politics*. New York: Crane Russak.

Katō, Shūjirō, ed. 1998. *Nihon no Anzen Hoshō to Kenpō* (Japanese National Security and the Constitution). Tokyo: Nansosha.

Katzenstein, Peter. 1996. *Cultural Norms and National Security*. Ithaca: Cornell University Press.

Keddell, Joseph. 1993. *The Politics of Defense in Japan*. Armonk, NY: M. E. Sharpe.

Kitaoka, Shinichi. 1999. "Kenpō Kyūjō no Jubaku kara Nukedasu Toki" (Time to Break the Spell of Article Nine). *This Is Yomiuri* (March): 126–35.

Kōsaka, Masataka. 1968. *Saishō Yoshida Shigeru* (Prime Minister Yoshida Shigeru). Tokyo: Chūō Kōronsha.

Krauss, Ellis, and Robert Pekkanen. 2004. "Explaining Party Adaptation to Electoral Reform: The Discreet Charm of the LDP?" *Journal of Japanese Studies* 30(1): 1–34.

Kunihiro, Masao. 1997. "The Decline and Fall of Pacifism." *Bulletin of Atomic Scientists* 53(1).

Layne, Christopher. 1993. "The Unipolar Illusion: Why New Great Powers Will Rise." *International Security* 17(4): 5–51.

LDP Special Study Group on Japan's Role in the International Community (LDP). 1992. "Japan's Role in the International Community–Draft Report." *Japan Echo* 19(2): 49–58.

Lind, Jennifer. 2004. "Pacifism or Passing the Buck? Testing Theories of Japanese Security Policy." *International Security* 29(1): 92–121.

Lutz, Donald. 1994. "Toward a Theory of Constitutional Amendment." *American Political Science Review* 88(2): 355–70.

MacArthur, Douglas. 1964. *Reminiscences: General of the Army.* New York: McGraw-Hill.

Maki, John M. 1962. *Government and Politics in Japan.* New York: Praeger.

————. 1964. *Court and Constitution in Japan.* Seattle: University of Washington Press.

Maruyama, Masao. 1963. *Thought and Behavior in Modern Japanese Politics.* Edited by Ivan Morris. London: Oxford University Press.

McNelly, Theodore. 1987. "Induced Revolution: The Policy and Process of Constitutional Reform in Occupied Japan." In Robert Ward and Yoshikazu Sakamoto, eds., *Democratizing Japan: The Allied Occupation.* Honolulu: University of Hawai'i Press.

Menon, Rajan. 1997. "The Once and Future Superpower." *Bulletin of Atomic Scientists* 53(1).

Miyazawa, Kiichi. 1997. "Rethinking the Constitution—a Document Tested by Time." *Japan Quarterly* 44(3).

Mochizuki, Mike M. 1997. "A New Bargain for a Stronger Alliance." In Mike M. Mochizuki, ed., *Toward a True Alliance: Restructuring U.S.-Japan Security Relations.* Washington, D.C.: Brookings Institution Press.

Nakamura, Akira. 2001. *Sengo Seiji ni Yureta Kenpō Kyūjō: Naikaku Hoseikyoku no Jishin to Tsuyosa* (Postwar Politics Under the Sway of Article Nine: The Confidence and Strength of the Cabinet Legislation Bureau). Tokyo: Chuokeizaisha.

National Institute for Defense Studies, ed. 2002. *East Asia Strategic Review, 2002.* Tokyo: National Institute for Defense Studies.

Nihon Bengoshi Rengōkai. 2005. "Kenpō Kaisei Kokumin Tōhyō Hōan ni Kansuru Ikensho" (Position Regarding the Constitutional Revision National Referendum Bill). Nihon Bengoshi Rengōkai (Japan Federation of Bar Associations), February 18. www.nichibenren.or.jp/jp/katsudo/sytyou/iken/05/2005_14.html.

Nishikawa, Shinichi. 2000. *Rippō no Chūsū: Shirarezaru Kanchō Naikaku Hōseikyoku* (The Center of Lawmaking: The Unknown Bureaucracy—The Cabinet Legislation Bureau). Tokyo: Satsuki Shobō.

Odawara, Atsushi. 1991. "The Kaifu Bungle." *Japan Quarterly* 38 (January–March): 6–14.

Ōtake, Hideo. 1988. *Saigunbi to Nashonarizumu* (Rearmament and Nationalism). Chūkōshinsho. Tokyo: Chūō Kōronsha.

———, ed. 2000. *Power Shuffles and Policy Processes.* Tokyo: Japan Center for International Exchange.

Packard, George. 1966. *Protest in Tokyo.* Princeton: Princeton University Press.

Purrington, Courtney. 1992. "Tokyo's Policy Response During the Gulf War and the Impact of the 'Iraqi Shock' on Japan." *Pacific Affairs* 65(2): 161–81.

Purrington, Courtney, and A. K. 1991. "Tokyo's Policy Responses During the Gulf Crisis." *Asian Survey* 31(4): 307–23.

Pyle, Kenneth. 1987. "In Pursuit of a Grand Design: Nakasone Betwixt the Past and the Future." *Journal of Japanese Studies* 13(2): 243–70.

———. 1996. *The Japanese Question.* Washington: AEI Press.

———. 1997. "Old New Orders and the Future of Japan and the United States in Asia." *IHJ Bulletin* 17(2).

Riddell, Peter. 2003. *Hug Them Close: Blair, Clinton, Bush, and the "Special Relationship."* London: Politicos.

Samuels, Richard J. 1994. *"Rich Nation, Strong Army": National Security and Japan's Technological Transformation.* Ithaca: Cornell University Press.

———. 2003a. *Machiavelli's Children: Leaders and Their Legacies in Italy and Japan.* Ithaca: Cornell University Press.

———. 2003b. "Leadership and Political Change in Japan: The Case of the Second Rinchō." *Journal of Japanese Studies* 29(1): 1–31.

———. 2004. "Politics, Security Policy, and Japan's Cabinet Legislation Bureau: Who Elected These Guys, Anyway?" Japan Policy Research Institute Working Paper 99 (March).

Samuels, Richard J., and J. Patrick Boyd. 2004. "Kenpō Kyūjō ni mo Kyūshō Ari?— Kenpō Ronsō no Yukue" (Does Article Nine Have Nine Lives?: The Future of the Constitutional Debate in Japan). *Ronza* (April): 174–83.

Schlichtmann, Klaus. 1995. "The Ethics of Peace: Shidehara Kikujirō and Article 9 of the Constitution." *Japan Forum* 7(1): 33–67.

Schoff, James, ed. 2004. *Crisis Management in Japan and the United States.* Washington, D.C.: Institute of Foreign Policy Analysis.

Shinoda, Tomohito. 2003. "Koizumi's Top-Down Leadership in the Anti-Terrorism Legislation: The Impact of Political Institutional Changes." *SAIS Review* 23(1): 19–34.

———. 2004. *Kantei Gaikō: Seiji Riidashippu no Yukue* (Prime Ministerial Foreign Policy: The Direction of Political Leadership). Tokyo: Asahi Shimbunsha.

Snyder, Glenn. 1984. "The Security Dilemma in Alliance Politics." *World Politics* 36(4): 461–95.

Stockwin, J. A. A. 1968. *The Japanese Socialist Party and Neutralism: A Study of a Political Party and Its Foreign Policy.* Melbourne: Melbourne University Press.

Twomey, Christopher. 2000. "Japan, a Circumscribed Balancer: Building on Defensive Realism to Make Predictions About East Asian Security." *Security Studies* 9(4): 167–205.

Unger, Danny. 1997. "Japan and the Gulf War: Making the World Safe for Japan-U.S. Relations." In Andrew Bennett, Joseph Lepgold, and Danny Unger, eds., *Friends in Need: Burden Sharing in the Persian Gulf War.* New York: St. Martin's Press.

Waltz, Kenneth. 1993. "The Emerging Structure of International Politics." *International Security* 18(2): 44–79.

———. 2000. "Structural Realism After the Cold War." *International Security* 25(1): 5–41.

Ward, Robert. 1965. "The Commission on the Constitution and Prospects for Constitutional Changes in Japan." *Journal of Japanese Studies* 24(3): 401–429.

Watanabe, Osamu. 2002. *Kenpō Kaisei no Sōten* (Issues of Constitutional Revision). Tokyo: Junpōsha.

Yamasaki, Taku. 2001. *Kenpō Kaisei* (Constitutional Revision). Tokyo: Seisansei.

Yoshida, Shigeru. 1962. *The Yoshida Memoirs: The Story of Japan in Crisis.* Boston: Houghton Mifflin.

Appendix

Partial Chronology of Incremental Shifts in Policy Guidelines and SDF Capabilities: 1980–2005

1981: Prime Minister Suzuki announces Japan will defend SLOCs up to 1,000 nautical miles.

1983: Nakasone government relaxes arms export restrictions to allow some technology transfers to the U.S.

1986: Nakasone government exceeds 1 percent of GNP ceiling for 1987 defense budget.

1991: Kaifu government deploys MSDF minesweepers to Persian Gulf in aftermath of first Gulf War.

1992: Diet passes PKO Law (International Peace Cooperation Law) allowing SDF participation in United Nations peacekeeping operations.

1995: Murayama government revises National Defense Program Outline to reorient SDF to post-Cold War threats.

1997: SDF officers achieve improved access to Cabinet Office and Ministers.

1998: Obuchi government relaxes ban on the military use of space by announcing acquisition plans for surveillance satellites.

1998: Obuchi government approves bilateral research on missile defense technologies with the U.S.

1999: Diet passes guideline laws allowing SDF to provide U.S. forces rear area support in the event of a regional emergency involving Japan's security.

2000–2005: SDF acquisition plans improve force projection capabilities, including aerial refueling and assault ships with carrier decks.

2001: Administrative reforms increase centralization of civilian control in the Prime Minister's Office.

2001: MSDF establishes a Special Forces unit for boarding/disarming ships.

2001: Diet passes Antiterrorism Law allowing the deployment of MSDF ships to Indian Ocean in support of coalition forces conducting operations in Afghanistan.

2001: Diet revises PKO Law relaxing use of weapons restrictions and unfreezing provisions restricting SDF participation in peacekeeping force (PKF) activities.

2002: Koizumi government deploys Aegis-equipped destroyer to Indian Ocean under Antiterrorism Law.

2003: Diet passes Emergency Measures Laws.

2003: Diet passes Iraq Reconstruction Law.

2004: GOJ fully implements SDF deployment to Iraq under Iraq Reconstruction Law.

2004: Diet approves measures to fund introduction of missile defense system.

2004: Koizumi government issues National Defense Program Guideline calling for new five-year buildup (2005–2010) of capabilities to engage in counterterrorism, defense of Japan's offshore islands, and surveillance of territorial waters.

2004: GSDF establishes Rapid Response Unit.

2004: Koizumi government eases arms export restrictions to allow technological cooperation with the U.S. on missile defense.

2005: Koizumi government approves possible transfer of joint U.S.-Japan developed missile defense system to third countries.

List of Reviewers 2004–05

The East-West Center Washington would like to acknowledge the following, who have offered reviews of manuscripts for *Policy Studies*.

Pamela Aall
United States Institute of Peace

Patricio Nunes Abinales
Kyoto University

Itty Abraham
Social Science Research Council, D.C.

Muthiah Alagappa
East-West Center Washington

Edward Aspinall
The University of Sydney

Robert Barnett
Columbia University

Gardner Bovingdon
Indiana University, Bloomington

Leslie Butt
University of Victoria

Craig Calhoun
New York University

Allen Carlson
Cornell University

Harold Crouch
Australian National University

Jay Dautcher
University of Pennsylvania

June Teufel Dreyer
University of Miami

Sumit Ganguly
Indiana University, Bloomington

Brigham Golden
Columbia University

Avery Goldstein
University of Pennsylvania

Reuel Hanks
Oklahoma State University

Eva-Lotta Hedman
University of Oxford

Paul Hutchcroft
University of Wisconsin, Madison

Sidney Jones
International Crisis Group

Yuen Foong Khong
Nuffield College, Oxford University

Stephanie Lawson
University of East Anglia

David Leheny
University of Wisconsin, Madison

R. William Liddle
The Ohio State University

Kenneth G. Lieberthal
University of Michigan

Thomas McKenna
SRI Consulting

Mike Mochizuki
The George Washington University

Andrew Nathan
Columbia University

Tashi Rabgey
Harvard University

Geoffrey Robinson
University of California, Los Angeles

Michael Ross
University of California, Los Angeles

Danilyn Rutherford
University of Chicago

Yitzhak Shichor
The Hebrew University of Jerusalem

Leonard Schoppa
University of Virginia, Charlottesville

Kirsten E. Schulze
London School of Economics

Sheldon Simon
Arizona State University

Timothy Sisk
University of Denver

Anthony Smith
Asia Pacific Center for Security Studies, Honolulu

Warren W. Smith
Radio Free Asia

Elliot Sperling
Indiana University, Bloomington

Arun Swamy
East-West Center

David Timberman
USAID, D.C.

Meredith Weiss
DePaul University

Geoffrey White
East-West Center

Policy Studies
Previous Publications

These issues of *Policy Studies* are presently available in print and online. Hardcopies
are available through Amazon.com. In Asia, hardcopies are available through the Institute
of Southeast Asian Studies, Singapore at 30 Heng Mui Keng Terrrace, Pasir Panjang
Singapore – 119614. Website: http://bookshop.iseas.edu.sg/

Online at: www.eastwestcenterwashington.org/publications